The Legend of Quail Lodge

Gary M. Koeppel

ISBN: 978-1-938924-08-8
Library of Congress Control Number: 2014940369
Edgar Haber Portrait: Jerry Van Megert
Cover Photo and Chapter Heading Photos: Rudy Quidileg
Historic and Golf Course Photos Courtesy of Quail Lodge
Design and Layout: Roger W. Rybkowski, Adpartner, Inc., www.myadpartner.biz

Coast Publishing
P.O. Box 223519
Carmel, CA 93922
831-625-8688
www.cstpub.com

Dedication

To Edgar and Terry Haber,
whose loving labors will inspire and nourish
those who follow for generations to come.

The Legend of Quail Lodge

One year after passing the torch of ownership to Peninsula Hotels in 1997, Edgar invited me to golf with Pierre Boppe, CEO of Peninsula Hotels and Nicklaus Leuenberger, GM, Peninsula New York. At the end of the round, as we passed through the pro shop en route to the 19th hole upstairs, I pointed out the empty alcove between the pro shop and stairs and suggested it would make a perfect place to display historic Quail memorabilia, photographs and trophies. To my surprise, Nick Leuenberger responded immediately, "Yes, let's do it!"

A month later an artist completed a rendering to illustrate what the History of Quail Lodge exhibits in the alcove area might look like, but the project was postponed because a major renovation was being planned for the clubhouse.

Two years later I was asked to research and digitally archive the history of Quail Lodge, then produce exhibition materials for the Grand Opening ceremonies planned for the 2006 completion of the hotel and clubhouse renovations. The exhibits included a series of large storyboard panels containing a pictorial history of the development of the golf course, home sites, clubhouse and hotel on the land of the original dairy farm. A selection of historic photographs were hung throughout Edgar's and the clubhouse and local artists were commissioned to create a bronze sculpture and portrait of founder Edgar Haber for permanent display at the foot of the grand stairway. A smaller version of the panel exhibits was published as a photo history book, though without any narrative.

For the past eight years I have been writing the book about the history of Quail Lodge and its founders. I interviewed more

Edgar and Terry Haber

than 80 people: golfers — both professionals and amateurs, employees and business associates, attorneys and bankers, fire and law enforcement officers, and friends and family members to gather information about Edgar and Terry Haber's lives, their passions and achievements in order to write this book, *The Legend of Quail Lodge.* This book was completed during the 50-year anniversary of the founding of Quail Lodge and Golf Club and it celebrates the legend created by the founders and the legacy they left behind.

How does a championship amateur golfer and a grade school teacher combine their heretofore unknown talents to convert a failing dairy farm into an award-winning golf course and resort? That was the key question posed to those who were a part of the successes; and their answers make up the substance of this book, the resulting content of which could be considered as an inspiration and manual for aspiring entrepreneurs and hoteliers.

Those golden years have now passed, but their glowing memories shine brightly: Terry Haber still nurtures her family, smaller now with kinsfolk not employees. And Nancy, who was Edgar's right arm, is now Terry's. Lawson has retired and is now practicing the art of leisure. The singing deputy DuVall is still talking story and Fire Chief Sidney Reade is putting out different kinds of fires. Rudy Quidileg is still mixing drinks in Edgar's, Denis Kerr is fixing a broken sprinkler somewhere, Mike Ochs is fixing something else somewhere else; and Bob Holmes is on the golf course fleecing friends in a friendly sort of way. And so many others of the Camelot Court are scattered here and there, but every single one remembers and holds dear their memories of the golden years.

Although the torch has passed, the essence of the founders' spirit lingers on. In the mind's eye, one can almost see Edgar in dapper clothes stepping out from a classic coupe and stooping down to pick up a discarded cigarette butt. One can imagine him in a meeting room with peers founding some new entity to help the people in the valley or, perhaps, one can get a glimpse of him putting on the practice green while mentoring a new employee. But most of all one remembers seeing him in his black and gold Mercedes station wagon rigged with emergency radios sputtering static and call numbers, rushing somewhere pell-mell with red light flashing and siren blaring to aid someone in distress.

However, one not need imagine Terry, Edgar's wife and more demure partner in life, because her mark of quality and delicate footprint is visible everywhere, from the lush landscaping to the elegant architecture of the lodge. One does wonder, however, with her kind and gentle ways, how she did manage to befriend so many, especially those who toiled for her, not as employees but as friends and family? Yes, to know those days, one wonders who, in fact, worked for whom.

And so the next time you tee up at the 17th, Edgar's favorite hole, take a moment to tip your cap in thanks to both Habers for what they have created and left behind for us to enjoy. And, from time to time, take a moment to enjoy the unspoiled beauty of the early morning dew glistening on the fairway grasses, or to feel the warm afternoon sun as it streams brightly through the nearby trees and hills beyond.

These are the moments when one senses the pervasive spirits of Edgar and Terry quietly watching over what they hath wrought, hoping we are enjoying our time here as much as they enjoyed theirs. And so we continue to savor the fruits of the Haber's loving labors, confident in knowing that generations to come will be forever nourished by what they have left behind.   — *Gary Koeppel*

This book explores how a golfer and schoolteacher, Edgar and Terry Haber, created the legacy that has become the Legend of Quail Lodge.
— Gary Koeppel

Edgar's favorite green, the signature 17th hole.

In Celebration of the Fifty-Year Anniversary

Quail Lodge and Golf Club 1964 to 2014

First Rounds

I thought golf was silly until the first time I swung at a golf ball and missed. Then I was hooked.

— Edgar Haber

AN ENTREPRENEUR IS BORN

Edgar Haber was born in 1912 in San Francisco to a merchant-class family whose father imported goods from Japan and whose mother ran the household.

Seven years before the 1906 earthquake and the subsequent fires that devastated the city from the Embarcadero waterfront to Van Ness Street, Edgar's father was on a steamship returning to San Francisco. When he returned, his family camped out in Golden Gate Park for a month before taking a ferry across the bay to safety.

"My mother told me it wasn't so much the earthquake," Edgar recalled, "it was that the water mains broke and there was no water to pump to put out the fires, so almost all of the buildings burned. When I was born six years later the city was still rebuilding."

Edgar's father imported things people needed, such as crude rubber in sticky blocks from South America that he sold to manufacturers for use in a variety of products, and Panama-style straw hats brought from Ecuador that he sold to Woolworth's and other stores. But before he became an importer, at 25 Edgar's father had sailed through the Inland Passage to Alaska to become a prospector digging for gold. He climbed the arduous Chilkoot Pass trail to reach the Klondike Gold Rush. But before anyone could enter the Klondike Territory to prospect for gold, the government of Canada required each prospector to haul 2,000 pounds of food and supplies that was needed to survive one year in the mining camps, which took many trips with heavy packs up the steep rocky trails. To move their supplies one linear mile forward the prospectors had to hike a distance of 80 miles, zigzagging up and down the rugged mountain trails.

After his moderately successful venture as a gold miner, Edgar's father journeyed to Mexico to work in an Antimony mine where he met a man who imported items

from the Orient. After taking a few trips with him as an associate, he decided to go into the importing business for himself, which he did for the rest of his life.

Edgar's grandfather on his mother's side was a porcelain dish maker in Dresden. When he immigrated to America he invested his savings of $10,000 in a small merchant company in San Diego. He became successful and civic minded, contributing generously to the San Diego Zoo and San Diego Symphony.

Edgar's mother oversaw a large family household that included his uncle and two aunts, both grandmothers, a nanny, Edgar and his brother, who died at an early age. "The nanny was a six-foot-two Scottish lady who told me that if I washed my hands, I'd be successful, because all successful business people washed their hands every day. And so, that stayed with me and I've never forgotten it," Edgar recalled.

GOLF IS A SILLY GAME

"When I was 17 and in high school, I did not play sports and had nothing to do after classes, so my grandmother would often take me to a hotel where I would play tennis," Edgar reflected. "But one day when no tennis players were around, a guy asked if I played golf. I had never even seen a golf course before, so I told him I thought it was a sissy game, whereupon he dared me to come to the golf course with him. A few days later I joined him at the course where he had been playing for years. I watched him hitting some balls on what he called a 'practice range,' which looked easy to me, so I borrowed one of his clubs, took a swing and missed it. Then I was hooked."

When Edgar told his father about discovering the game of golf during the trip to the golf course with his friend, his father said he had a friend, Chuck Sprokens, who was a golf pro and he encouraged Edgar to go to his golf studio. Edgar took the Montgomery Street Trolley for 5¢ to where the golf pro taught. The instructor asked him to hit some shots into an indoor net. Apparently impressed, the pro told him, "Well, I'll teach you, but only if you practice your golf swing every day."

So every afternoon, six days a week, Edgar took the trolley across town and hit golf balls into the net. Every night, after his schoolwork was done, he practiced his golf swing in his room, over and over again, for hundreds of times every evening, until his swing became smooth, "almost silken," as his instructor would say. Every week on Sundays, his golf coach took him to a nearby public course where they would play 18 holes. "I shot 130 the first day but, as I practiced hard and played more, I eventually got my handicap down to a 2."

After graduating from high school, Edgar's marks were not high enough to attend college, so he attended a business college for a year and a half, during which time he continued to practice and play golf. Because he did not like gym classes, he joined the high school Reserve Officer's Training Corps, the ROTC, and became a lieutenant, which would serve him well years later when he enlisted in the Army after the attack on Pearl Harbor.

While studying business he continued to play golf and improved his game. He wrote down every stroke and studied every scorecard; he paid particular attention to the number of putts he made.

GOLF IS A GREAT GAME

At age 20, three years after his first swing and miss that hooked him into playing golf, Edgar qualified to play in the 1933 San Francisco Amateur Golf Championship at the TPC Harding Park Municipal Golf Club. There, beside the beautiful freshwater Lake Merced in Southwest San Francisco, surrounded by lush vegetation and towering Monterey Cypress Trees, Edgar played in his first golf tournament. In a field of 1,481 players and in front of 5,000 spectators, the championship round came down to the final match between renowned golf veteran Whiting Walters and an unknown young amateur named Edgar Haber.

THE GOLF GODMOTHER

"When I think about what I ever did in my life to get where I am today, any money I ever made was because I played golf. By good fortune, I played pretty well, and winning the city championship put my name around a little bit.

"My Godmother lived in Monterey. Jobs were hard to come by after the depression and before the war. I had nothing else to do so I would come down to Carmel, visit her for a few days and play golf wherever and whenever I could.

"I knew about the state championship golf tournament that was held every year in Monterey. For $5 — if you had $5 — you could enter the tournament at Pebble Beach. It took two rounds to qualify, one at Pebble Beach and the other at Cypress Point. So for five bucks you got two rounds on beautiful golf courses, and if you won a flight you got another round. Even if you lost there was a consolation flight, so you could play again. If you won the third you played for the fourth day. That was a lot of golf for five bucks, if you had it.

"I always played during the week, on Mondays, Wednesdays and Fridays. I never played on the weekends because it was harder to sneak on, which I did because

Proving Golf Match Never Lost Until Last Putt Drops

by A. D. Mills, Sports Writer, *San Francisco Chronicle*

While many veterans and youngsters were tasting defeat, young Haber and the veteran Walters kept right on winning matches by playing superb golf and eventually reached the stage where they faced each other in the decider.

The opening nine holes of play found Walters shooting in the better-than-par form and he made the first turn with a 3-up lead over his youthful opponent. Continuing to display the same fine brand of golf on the incoming half of the morning round, Whitey added another hole to give him a 4-up lead at the half way post. Quite a nice appetizer for lunch, eh?

Now, whether or not that lay-off for lunch was or was not the cause of the sudden change in Walters' golf in the afternoon is not known to the writer (nor anyone else, probably) but it was decidedly 'sour,' especially on the outward journey where he lost hole after hole, and when the pair teed-off at the three quarter post, young Mr. Haber had not only wiped out the 4-down leeway but was holding the lead by a 2-up advantage.

Twas a distinct surprise for everyone present, as it was thought that the veteran had the match and the championship safely tucked away when the morning round had ended.

Both players fought hard and played rather well, especially on recovery shots, on the last lap of the journey, and it looked as though the match would go the full 36 holes until Haber holed a 16-footer on the 17th green (the 35th hole of the match) for a halve of the hole and a two and one win of the match and title.

Edgar Haber's photo filled half of the front page of the San Francisco Chronicle Sporting Green *on March 22, 1933, with a bold headline.*

When Edgar stepped up to the podium to accept the coveted San Francisco City Championship trophy, his father stood beside him to share the moment.

Haber Captures City Golf Championship

San Francisco Chronicle Sporting Green, March 23, 1933

Three years after he first gripped a club and found out for himself that there is a difference between a mashie and a driver, 20-year-old Edgar Haber yesterday became San Francisco city golf champion.

Starting his bid for the title as the darkest of dark horses, the tall, slender youngster finished like a thoroughbred to defeat the veteran Lincoln Parker, E. H. Whiting Walters, in a shower-soaked, wind-blown final at Harding Park.

Imperturbable in the face of rushing galleries and Walters' brilliant morning golf, Haber met every qualification of a champion by counting back to wipe out the four down handicap and cinch victory at last by poking down a fifteen-foot putt on the thirty-fifth green.

Unrattled by what appeared to be impossible odds and thinking only of the methodical form which he has acquired by three years of intensive practice, Haber came back in the afternoon with an exhibition of steady golf that won him six holes in a row and seven of the after round's first nine.

1933 trophy

I was broke and didn't have a job. At the time, Pebble Beach didn't care so much about getting paid on weekdays as they did on weekends when everyone wanted to golf.

"Memories of golfing on the Monterey Peninsula stayed with me. I visited my Godmother as much as I could and played as much golf as possible until one day when my father said it was time to get a job and earn some money."

GOLFING IN WAIKIKI

After winning the San Francisco championship, the country was still in the throes of the Great Depression, which had begun in 1929 and bottomed in 1932, but the economic hardships continued for years to come. Edgar's father got him a job as a Steward on a steamship to Hawaii.

"I didn't do very well at that, I got seasick on the way over, and so when we got to Hawaii, which took four-and-a-half very long days to get there, I'd had enough of the life of a seaman and got off the boat in Honolulu. I had only $11 in my pocket, which was a lot then, but when I telegraphed my family for more, they

One of Edgar Haber's favorite golf courses in Hawaii.

didn't have any to send because the depression continued to hit everyone hard, so I was on my own.

"I found a place on Waikiki to rent for $30 a month, a shack right on the beach. Every morning I'd crawl out my window and go swimming in the warm clear water that — for some reason that I could never figure out — made my landlord a little unhappy, so I soon found a nicer place for less money, though it wasn't on the water.

"When playing golf one day, I met a man who owned an automobile dealership and he offered me a job selling cars. Every day, after spending most of the day trying to sell cars, in the afternoons I'd take one of their cars to the golf course and play. I didn't know anybody in Hawaii, so it was hard to sell cars as a stranger to a stranger.

"Every day I'd swim a little, try to sell some cars, and then go out to the golf course. Sometimes a guy would say, you know, how much are we playing for? And we'd talk a little, get the terms agreed on, and then go at it. Sometimes I'd lose, but usually I won, though it was never more than anyone could comfortably lose. I wasn't a shark; you know, a golf shark, though there are a few of them out there.

"I tried hard to sell cars, but I wasn't very inspired. I think I only sold one car the entire time I worked for the dealership. Then one day I got sick and collapsed, so I booked passage on a ship and sailed back to San Francisco."

When Edgar returned to the San Francisco, he learned his parents had lost their home and were renting a house designed by Julia Morgan, who was William Randolph Hearst's private architect who designed his castle in San Simeon. He recalled it wasn't a large or very fancy house, but very comfortable in its design, and it was something his father could afford.

It was hard to find a job during the depression years. One of his girl friend's fathers gave him a job sweeping floors in a factory for 50¢ an hour. "On Sundays she would invite me for dinners of prime rib and cooked bread, great food, but I sat at the far end of the table facing her father, who didn't like me because I was a four-bit-an-hour employee and the boyfriend of his daughter. Although her mother was nice to me, he was a little rough because, you know, I didn't quite fit the pattern, economically, so to speak."

At 29 Edgar had been married for two years and had one child, which were conditions that could have exempted him from military service, but instead of exercising the exemption, the day after the Japanese attacked Pearl Harbor he enlisted in the Army. Edgar told the recruiter he had served in the ROTC, "so I started as a second Lieutenant, which was pretty good," he recalled modestly. When asked about his military experience, he said he was stationed in the South Pacific and assigned to ships that delivered supplies to soldiers who were serving duty on nearby, but remote, islands for so long they thought they had been forgotten, at least until the supply ships came in with new provisions.

When I think about what I ever did in my life to get where I am today, any money I ever made was because I played golf.
— Edgar Haber

The Monocular

You can't par them all unless you par the first one.

— *Edgar Haber*

THE MONOCULAR, OR SPORTS SCOPE

"My first venture into business was after I was reassigned to San Francisco but still in the Army. Harry, a fellow I knew pretty well, asked me one day if I could loan him $10. He offered me a weird thing to hold until he could pay me back. It looked like a binocular, except it was a monocular — because it had one magnifying scope instead of two. He said he had made it himself with parts from army surplus that were hard to get during the war but plentiful now that the war was over. It was nine powers in strength. It looked nice, all aluminum and shiny, and when you looked through it with one eye it worked pretty well in magnifying distant things.

"During my first day on leave I took this thing into a camera store and asked for the owner. 'What could you sell this for?'"

"Where did you get that?" he asked

I just said, "We make them," even though the fellow made it, not "we," and it was the only one, not "them."

"Well, I like it," he replied, "What do you call it?"

"I didn't want to say it was a nine-power, fifty-millimeter monocular in spun aluminum that nobody had ever seen before because it was the first one ever, so I said, 'It's a Sporting Scope.'"

"How much are they?"

"I really had no idea, so I asked how much he could sell it for, and he said, '$75.'"

"I knew there was a 50% discount because I'd done other things like that. If someone wanted a refrigerator, I had found out where you could buy one wholesale and I could make some money on the deal from the difference."

"I can sell them to you for $47.50 each," I told him. "Then I'll take a dozen for the first order," he replied.

"When I returned to base I told Harry, the fellow who made the monocular, that I had just sold 12 of them! At first he was excited, then he got a little panicked. He said he had made only one in his entire life, and this one was made from scrap military materials, and it would take some figuring and some seed money to buy materials to make more of them. 'Well, how much,'" I asked him.

"He figured it would take 20 bucks each for materials. By that time I was Captain in the Army and made $350 a month, which wasn't so bad because they fed you and put you up, so there weren't many expenses unless you drank, which I didn't, so I put up the money and Harry made the first dozen monoculars, that is, Sporting Scopes.

"The camera store quickly sold out the first batch and ordered more, and I thought that maybe I had a business going, so I went back to Harry and told him I had an order for 24 more.

"Harry about flipped. He didn't know how to make so many. So I figured we needed a lathe and someone who could do the optics. We were still at war and the materials were still hard to find those days, but we began finding discarded army surplus parts and then found some ladies who had done similar work for the service to polish them up. Soon I found an old abandoned store in San Francisco that we rented for $50 per month and that's where we assembled and polished the monoculars.

"So it turned out to be a pretty good business. Whenever I got a day off I would call on a camera store and sell more Sporting Scopes until the sales slowed down. One day, while passing by Bulloch and Jones, a men's clothing store, I saw some shiny knives in the window, so I went inside, but when I asked the manager if he would sell the monoculars, he replied adamantly that he was not interested.

"I asked, 'will you take a couple on consignment and put them in the window with the knives, then pay me when they sold?' Still reluctant, he finally agreed, and soon he was reordering Sporting Scopes every couple of weeks or so.

"The Scopes became very popular but if it were to succeed beyond San Francisco, a sales force would be needed to distribute them, which required salesmen, travel expenses and other costs. So I figured, every day guys were transferring to a new outfit somewhere across the country, so I'd give them a free sample Sporting Scope so on their days off they could take them around to that area's camera stores, clothing stores, sporting goods and department stores located near the base where they were stationed.

"In time the Sport Scopes were distributed from San Francisco to New York and from the Philippines to Australia, from optical stores to hardware stores to department stores to sporting goods dealers. The distribution system worked well and it was free.

"They sold dozens of them over and over again, as did other stores, so by the time I got through, I'd sold thousands of them. Then it appeared that the war was about to be over and there would be plenty of optics available and no army soldiers to sell and distribute them, so I sold the business for about $15,000, I think.

"That was the first bit of money that I ever made. I guess it was a lot of luck."

THE MIMEOGRAPH

"When the war was over I was still in uniform for another 90 days. My wife and I moved off base into an inexpensive 5,000-unit apartment development called Park Merced where a lot of military families lived. When we moved in we tried to buy some furniture but you couldn't find any because everything was still

scarce after the war. One day I went into the common laundry room and discovered a bulletin board filled with paper signs of every shape and color, tacked, stapled and scotch taped on the bulletin board, such as, 'Shipping out Next Week, Must Sell This or That, Furniture for Sale Good Price, Nice Car for Sale,' and so on.

"So I rented a used typewriter and borrowed a used mimeograph machine and started a little newspaper called the *Park Merced News,* a mimeo-sheet, full of little classified ads that said you can sell your stuff if you place an ad here. Everyone seemed to be either moving in or shipping out from the apartment complex. People would place ads to get rid of their stuff while others would line up for the next edition because they knew they could buy whatever they needed at prices that were almost nothing. Everybody won.

"When this little sheet was making about $400 per month, I sold it."

THE CARMEL VALLEY SUN

"Everything I did seemed to come from golf or be about golf. After the war I played golf as much as possible, which included many trips to the Monterey Peninsula, home of some the best golf courses in the world. I didn't have a job and liked the area. In fact I enjoyed it so much, and to be closer to the golf courses, I eventually moved to Carmel Valley, which at that time was filled with horses and cows, cowboys and farmers.

"When I arrived I had no job, but I saw the same needs as I did with the mimeograph sheet in San Francisco, so I started Carmel Valley's first newspaper, the *Carmel Valley Sun,* that advertised everything from baby sitters to bath tubs and also reported on local news and events. There was no other publication in the area, so as with the Lake Merced mimeo sheet, it provided a needed service in the community."

THE LIQUOR STORE

"Then I looked around for what else Carmel Valley did not have, and one was a liquor store. A golfer friend got me a job with a wholesale liquor company and after awhile sales were pretty good so I rented an empty store way out in the remote village for $75 a month. The building owner was a very prominent person who knew everybody. He saw it as a great business opportunity and wanted to be a 50-50 partner in the venture and insisted on a buy/sell agreement, so we both put up $2,500 and opened the store.

"A year later the store had become very profitable and the partner asked to buy me out, so I said I'd think about it. After considering his offer over the weekend, I told him I had decided not to sell and would keep my share. He became upset and claimed I had agreed to sell to him, which I hadn't, but rather than have him believe that I had welched on my word, I told him if that's what he thought I said, then I would back out and sell my interest to him. When I met with his attorney, the well-known Carmel Martin, Sr., he somehow figured out that I really hadn't agreed to sell and understood my thinking that since the partner thought I did, that I would rather sell than have him think I broke my word. I guess he knew his client pretty well and seemed to think I was in the right and an okay guy. Years later Carmel Martin's son would recall this experience to me when I bought a dairy farm.

"I wondered what else was needed in Carmel Valley. Whenever people in Carmel Valley wanted to go to a movie, they had to drive to Monterey. There was no movie theatre in the Valley. Great idea, I thought. So I asked around and learned you could rent a movie on a 16mm reel pretty cheap, so I found an empty old barn, rented it for $50 a month, cleaned it out, bought some chairs and turned it into a movie theatre. I sold tickets for 50¢ and thought I'd make a killing, but I learned that people preferred driving to Monterey to watch movies, and so the theater idea flopped.

"Between the newspaper and liquor store, I was earning about $600 per month and was able to get enough time off to golf on Mondays, Wednesdays and Fridays. But after selling both businesses and closing the theatre, once again I was out of work and started looking around.

"One day during a round of golf, a friend who was a golfer introduced me to a fellow player, the manager of a life insurance company, Equitable Life in Monterey, and I wound up going to work for them selling insurance and home mortgages. Their office was in an old building and the furnishings were frayed and kinda musty, and I could see our clients were not impressed when they visited. I was only a salesperson, but I told them their office was not very presentable and that I could build them a new building, which I had never done before, and to my surprise they agreed.

"So I bought a small lot on the corner in Monterey, built the building and leased it to them until I eventually sold it. In the meantime, because I'd gotten to know the real estate business, from the lending side I learned how much you could borrow and on the selling side I learned about how much houses were worth. So I got into real estate, bought and sold a few homes and made a small profit on each one. I had a bunch on little real estate deals like that and they kept getting bigger."

Edgar's second experience in building was the King's Lodge at the bottom of the hill on Munras Street in Monterey for a British couple, the Knaptons, who ran it for years before retiring. Years later when he built Quail Lodge, Edgar was so impressed with the way they had operated their motel that he hired Mr. Knapton to become the first manager of the lodge.

The Handshake

The best things that have ever happened to me happened because of golf.

— *Edgar Haber*

A HANDSHAKE FOR A DAIRY FARM

"The three children from my first wife were all attending schools in Carmel Valley and one day, their teacher — Mrs. Terry Jones, the lady who was to become at first my assistant and then my business partner, wife and love of my life — took them on a field trip to a dairy farm. As a parent I was invited. The barns, which I liked, were full of bales of hay. The grazing area was bottomland beside the wooded banks of the Carmel River and was filled with dairy cows feeding in large fields of green grass surrounded by white picket fencing.

"I thought it was the most beautiful piece of land I had ever seen. But I didn't see a dairy farm. All I could see was a golf course. Fairways and greens. Doglegs and straightaways. Three, four and five par holes. And lots of lakes carved in the flats and natural furrows. A golf course, not a dairy farm.

"I didn't get the name of the man showing us around and didn't know if he was the manager or owner or cow-milker. During the tour I said, 'Boy, I sure would like a place like this someday.' You know, that was kinda crazy because I was only making about $600 a month by working two jobs. The man didn't reply or say much, just nodded his head and went on with the tour.

One of the original barns on the Morrow Dairy Farm.

View of future 11th hole fairway.

"I didn't know until 10 years later that the dairy tour guide was Dwight Morrow, the brother of Anne Lindbergh, who spoke in long sentences and large words because he had been an English professor at Harvard before becoming a dairy farmer. I also didn't know that his brother-in-law, the famous American aviator, Charles Lindbergh, often came to Carmel Valley just to stay at the dairy farm to get away from people because of his notoriety from the kidnap and murder of his baby son.

"About 10 years later, Mr. Morrow called me and asked if I was still interested in buying his dairy farm. I could have fallen over, but I was able to tell him that, yes, I was interested, but you know, how much did he want. He gave me a price that sounded pretty good to me, so I took a deep breath and told him that I would like to have it, though I had no idea where I'd get that kind of money to buy it.

"Some time later he called again and asked if I was still interested, which I was, and then asked if I minded being asked a personal question, namely 'what do you do for a living?' In other words, he was asking if I could afford to buy his property. When I told him I sold insurance, he checked me out with the company and bank to see how I was doing and found out I was doing pretty well and had a good name, so he called me back he said he would sell it to me but had to have an appraisal done.

"At that point I figured I had no chance because I had been told the price he had originally quoted me was way below the current value of $1,200 per acre for dairy land for the 245 acres, or about $300,000. He said he wanted $50,000 down and gave me three years to pay the balance, but I had only $10,000 so I got a couple of friends together and told them it was a wonderful piece of land, didn't know exactly yet what to do with it, but it was worth far more than he was asking, so each of them put up $10,000 and we had the down payment.

"Little did I know at the time that Mr. Morrow's attorney was the son of Carmel Martin, Sr., who knew about me from his father and the liquor store deal years before. He told Mr. Morrow, 'Well, my dad says he's okay.' When I went into his office, he asked the name of my attorney, but I didn't need one because the deal was so simple. Mr. Martin, Jr. asked me several times in several ways if I really wanted to buy the dairy farm, and each time I assured him I wanted to buy it and had a check for $50,000 for the down payment in my pocket.

"When Mr. Martin reminded me that we did not have a purchase agreement or anything in writing, that all I had was a conversation and a handshake, I thought I was sunk.

"After even more questions about my interest and ability, he finally asked for my check, then he sighed and opened his desk drawer from which he pulled out a check for $100,000. My heart sank again.

"He said, 'This check is a down payment for twice as much as you've offered for the price of the dairy farm, but Mr. Morrow told you he would sell it to you for the price you two had agreed upon, and that he will not accept another offer even if it was for more money. Mr. Morrow said you are a man who keeps his word and so does he. The dairy farm is yours.'"

THE BANKER FROM CYPRESS POINT

"The four gentlemen who invested with me in the purchase of the Dairy Farm in 1960 were all good businessmen and sharp money managers. When they

View of the north west grazing field.

asked what my plans were for developing the property, I said it was a great piece of land at a good price and would make a beautiful golf course, to which they burst out in uncontrollable laughter. They didn't want anything to do with a golf course because they said it was a lousy business and would lose money. Instead, they insisted, it was prime flat land, well situated, and zoned for 250 homes that they thought they could easily get rezoned to increase the density to 500 homes. They figured at a cost of only $500 a lot, they could sell them for $15,000 each and make a killing.

"The idea of seeing that beautiful dairy farm land with a river meandering through it turned into a subdivision of houses squeezed together was quite a different view from mine, which was to create a beautiful golf course and keep most of the land in some kind of protected open space or scenic easement. But also I didn't want them to lose anything for helping me with purchasing the land, so I offered to buy them out to make them whole. One of them wanted to stay in so we offered to buy out the other two, who wound up making a good profit in a short time. So everyone was happy.

"Now we had the land but not nearly enough money to build a golf course, so we went around to all of our friends and their friends asking them to invest, but that didn't work out so well. I had only one option left. A golfing friend had a friend who was a friend of a member of the board of Crocker Bank. Usually a local bank will send a local loan application to San Francisco so when it's rejected they don't have a public relations problem. Somehow or other my friend arranged for me to talk directly with a member of the board at the local branch, which was unheard of at the time.

"So I put on my only suit and went to the bank for a loan. The bank manager was retiring and when I arrived he had asked the board to hear my case directly which, again, was unheard of. I knew that the chairman of the bank was also on the board of the Cypress Point Golf Club and I was pretty nervous when he asked what I wanted a loan for, and I said: 'It's probably the worst investment you can make, it's a golf course and they all lose money except yours.'

"He looked startled and he asked me what I meant by my comment. I said to him that a player can barely get on Cypress, because your club is private where only members play except for a few non-members, which you allow to play, and from them your club earns enough to pay most of your expenses. It only takes three or four foursomes a day at $400 per foursome to pay the bills. He was shocked and asked how I knew that. I said, 'Well, I thought I'd better find out before I came here.' So, he asked, 'how would you make a profit with a golf course in Carmel Valley?' And I said, 'Well, your golf course is a secret; I intend to make mine not a secret. I want a business, so I'll let it be known to everyone everywhere.'

"To that the chairman did not have much else to say except, 'Okay, here's the dough and good luck.' and I left the bank with a commitment for enough money to build a golf course."

LADY QUAIL: THE PARTNER FROM HEAVEN

Before launching into the story about Edgar's creation of the golf course, clubhouse, fairway homes and hotel, it is fitting to introduce the woman who at first assisted Edgar and then married him to become his partner for life as well as being an integral part of every visual aesthetic and every employee relationship on the properties they were to build together.

Terry Jones was the only child of a lettuce farmer and schoolteacher in San Diego. She obtained a teaching degree at Pomona College before moving to the Monterey Peninsula where she taught 4th grade in Pacific Grove, Carmel and for the last 10 years of her teaching career, in Carmel Valley where she met Edgar. Quite coincidentally, Terry taught grade school to all of Edgar's three children from his first marriage.

Although Edgar was the master of finance and making money, Terry was the mistress of spending what he earned — but with remarkable good taste that helped create the successes of the operations.

Terry worked closely with the architect, Charlie Rose, and the landscaper, Charlie Hough, both of whom turned out to be exactly what the project needed to succeed. She selected the trees that were planted throughout the golf course and all of the landscaping for the clubhouse and lodge. She oversaw the architectural designs and interiors for the clubhouse and hotel, and selected the materials, fabric, colors and textures that a short time later became a large part of the reason that Quail Lodge earned the Five-Star Mobil Award for Excellence.

We fought over budgets like cats and dogs, but in the end Edgar always chose quality over mediocrity, even if we had to work a lot harder to pay for it. We always said, 'He made the money, and I spent it.' It was a very good combination. Well, I mean we spent it all on business. We used to go around and around about it because I would want to spend money and he always would not want to spend it. I didn't have to go through channels and committees, but I did have to get it by him, which wasn't always easy, but when I could jar him loose with the money, he was always glad afterwards.

— Terry Haber

for an unprecedented 20 years. As she often said, "good taste is free and excellence doesn't cost much more."

But Terry's modesty mirrored Edgar's. She always credited other people for their talents, for the quality of the development and for its successes in excellence. She claims her best contribution was in the selection of the right professionals: the architect, the interior designer and the landscape designer. Both Terry and Edgar sang the praises of others, never themselves.

Without Terry Haber one wonders how Edgar would have ever managed. While he was the expert on business matters and operations, her talent was in her

---

Many good things happened to Mr. Haber, but Terry Haber was the very best thing that ever happened to him.
— Bonny Chapman

THE $1,000 CHAIR
My dad always complained about Terry spending money.
She could pick out 12 chairs and line them up in the dining room.
It didn't matter whether they cost $100 or $1000. It didn't register
with her. She always selected the one she wanted, 'the appropri-
ate one.' It drove my dad nuts. He wanted the $100 dollar deal.
She wanted the best chair with the best design and the best color
that was right for the use she had in mind. But once she made her
choice, he always backed her up and paid the piper because he,
too, wanted the best. Together they were a great combination.
— John Haber Splittorf

---

uncanny ability to select the right people for the right job and to have the right aesthetics for the right application. Together, from a Carmel Valley Dairy Farm, they created what became an award-winning golf and country club and an internationally known a Five-Star Resort.

EDGAR'S DAYTIME WIFE

Edgar used to say he had two wives, one daytime and one nighttime, and he often mused, "on a golf course I can recall every player's shot on every hole and the running score of each, but without Nancy I can't tell you who I'm supposed to meet with tomorrow."

The more I worked for Edgar on the aesthetics of every aspect of the project, the more I became more involved — in more ways than one — and, gradually, at some point, we had fallen in love and got married. So we became personal partners as well as partners in creating a whole new business — something neither one of us had ever done before.
— Terry Haber

Terry always helped Edgar see things in a different perspective and brought out the softer side in him. Quail Lodge was like a big family. They knew everything about the employees — who had children, who had died, who was sick — really, everything about everyone. They honored their employees with festive Christmas parties for the entire family members and they hosted Five-Star dinners to honor five-year employees and to award them Five-Star pins for service. Terry was the person who kept everyone else together.
— Carmen Ajan

Typical Quail Lodge room with unique decor.

transferred them into his appointment book. He dictated his correspondence to Nancy who took notes in shorthand, then submitted him the draft for review. He would often remark, "Nancy, we write a good letter together!"

Mr. Haber was kind, funny, clever and sometimes frustrating but always nice. He never hesitated to help people in any way he could, financial or otherwise. I kept track of all of his appointments and I used to stick post-its on his lapel so he would remember his meeting, except for his tee times, which he never needed a reminder because he never forgot when he was supposed to play golf. When he needed to know something that took some research, together we learned how to be 'private eyes' and became such good sleuths we could investigate almost anything or anyone. He was a frustrated FBI guy, you know.
— Nancy Parsons

Nancy Parsons was the person who kept Edgar Haber's complex life organized — at least during the daytime. From 1979 she worked for Edgar for 26 years during his lifetime and four more after he passed. As his Girl Friday Every Day, Nancy served as his personal secretary, events assistant, go-to person, office door guard, *Quail Trails* and *Quail Talk* editor and the country club membership sales manager and coordinator.

As Terry Haber was Lady Quail, Nancy was Sister Quail, as they were fondly called. Terry was Edgar's nighttime wife and Nancy was is daytime wife. The two wives kept the Chief Quail organized and in one piece as he evolved into an accomplished, first-time developer of a golf course, country club subdivision and hotel.

Nancy Parsons was the Keeper of the Gate. She knew who had easy access and who needed to be approved for access. Every morning she recalls meeting in his office to review the day's calendar. Edgar always made countless notes on post-its and stuck them wherever they would stick until she gathered and

Terry Haber's Covey decor featured unique objects.

Pastures Into Fairways

To layout the holes in the cow pasture, from wher- ever my drive landed I stepped off 30 paces for the roll, and where the chip landed became the center of the green.

— *Edgar Haber*

From the first day he swung a golf club to winning the San Francisco City Championship to golfing three days a week most of his life, Edgar Haber was first and foremost a golfer. He loved the game and enjoyed playing it as a game. He was an exceptional golfer with a memorable golf swing to those who understood. And after all the variety of things he had done to earn a living, with

Terry and the Haber children exploring the dairy farm.

nearly 30 years having passed since his first championship victory, at age 48 Edgar's time had finally come: he was going to design his own golf course.

He was exhilarated by his dreams for the dairy farm but challenged by the daunting tasks that lay ahead. He pondered about which part of the dream to build first, the golf course and clubhouse or home sites and hotel. He loved the natural beauty of the old dairy farm and often spoke with his daughters, Anne and Marilyn, about preserving the property for posterity. During the development process, he decided to dedicate the entire golf course in perpetuity to a scenic open space and conservation easement so that nothing inappropriate could ever spoil its rural character and natural beauty.

Edgar mused, "At the time, banks had a lot of skepticism about developers in California, that's what we came to be called then, developers — not builders, perhaps because some builders had used the promise of including a golf course when they only wanted to develop lots and sell home sites, but then they would run out of money and didn't have funds to build the golf course, so they would renege on their promise. We decided it was best to build the golf course and the subdivision at the same time, then the clubhouse and hotel. But above all I loved the old dairy farm; it was pure, simple, natural beauty at its best, and I wanted to retain as much of its native look as possible."

GREENING OF THE GREENBELT

I can remember walking down to the Carmel River and fishing with my dad and listening to him talk about how beautiful the dairy farm was and hoping the land would always stay as natural as possible. He often spoke about preserving the natural beauty in a green belt, or some kind of scenic easement, so it could never be torn up, which I didn't understand at the time. While dad was building the golf course, I used to love working for him, doing whatever help his secretary needed. I listened to all of the excited conversations, especially how they were protecting the property by creating a golf course instead of turning it into a giant subdivision, which is what one of my dad's first partners had wanted for the property. As it turns out my dad was aware of conservation long before it became popular and a part of everyone else's thinking. He was like that, always ahead of his time.

— Anne Haber

THE GOLFER AND GOLF COURSE DESIGNER

Edgar explained what qualities he was looking for in a professional golf course designer. "I was a pretty good golfer and planned to be very involved in the golf course design, but knew I needed to find a golf course designer with a small enough ego so we could work together and not a big name so I would be able to afford him. I interviewed quite a few good designers before meeting Robert Muir Graves."

Graves had graduated in Landscape Architecture from the University of California at Berkeley in 1953. He was a student of the renowned British golf course designer, Alister MacKenzie, who taught him "the chief object of every golf course architect worth his salt is to imitate the beauties of nature."

By 1959 Graves' office was devoted exclusively to golf course design, but he had been designing only 9-hole golf courses before meeting Edgar Haber and bidding on the Quail golf course, which was his first 18-hole project. Edgar recognized young talent and high energy as well as his pleasant personality and his willingness to work together to create the golf course.

Edgar and his golfing friend and realtor, Jim May, could be seen hitting golf balls on the dung-littered, weed-infested dairy pasture during the early months of planning. Anyone passing by would have raised their eyebrows at seeing two grown men hitting golf balls in the dairy fields. Wherever their best drives landed, hopefully between cow droppings, they would step off 30 yards for the roll that would have happened with the ball on a fairway, and then they chipped their second shot and wherever it landed became the center of the green.

Although knowing they needed to plan a subdivision around the periphery of the course, which was a new concept that Jack Nicklaus's company was also beginning to develop, both Edgar and Robert Graves collaborated with a concept that put the golf course first and the home sites second. Neither man would allow his priorities to be compromised.

PRESERVING A FARM AND A FOREST
My husband and I migrated to Mendocino and lived an alternative lifestyle quite unlike my father's. But when I would visit him we talked a lot about trees, water and conserving resources. I think the way he saved the dairy farm land by creating an open space for the golf course rather than building a dense housing development inspired me to live a life of conservation. We spent long hours discussing the devastating logging practices of Maxxam that had just bought out the Pacific Lumber Company in Northern California, which for over a hundred years had practiced sustainable logging methods of forest management. Maxxam turned out to be an irresponsible reaper instead of Pacific's careful stewardship. My dad shared my concerns and was a very thoughtful developer.
— Marilyn Haber

COLLABORATIVE CREATIVITY
When Mr. Haber was selecting an architect, he didn't want to have a big name architect. He wanted to have somebody who was fresh and young and full of great, innovative ideas but also somebody who he could have a good working relationship with so that there was good communication between the two. As a superb amateur golfer himself, Mr. Haber needed to have an active part of the design process. And my dad was good at working with people in that way. He didn't waltz in and say this is the only way that you can layout this course. And he knew that Mr. Haber wanted to be a part of the design process, which I think was one of the main reasons why they got along so well.
— Virginia Graves

GOLFING IN THE PASTURE

It was something to see two grown men playing golf in the pasture. They would stand at high points trying to see what was there, asking what can you do from here and what kind of club would you use from there, and that sort of thing. They had a marvelous time golfing in the pasture. They'd stand up on the hill where the dairy farmer had his farmhouse, where the condos are now above the 5th green, which we turned into our first office. They stood on top of that hill and planned where the fairways and greens and lakes should be located. Those were exciting times for Edgar.

— Terry Haber

Edgar Haber posing for a photo at the future 11th tee.

Edgar Haber and Jim May laying out Quail golf course in the dairy farm fields.

ABOVE EVERY THING ELSE

Forty-some years have passed and I am still designing and redesigning golf courses. When I think back about all the people who had enough faith in me to support my efforts, Ed Haber's name is at the top of the list. I soon learned how fortunate I was to be working for a client who put the golf course and game of golf above everything else. After many projects combining golf with other facilities, such as residences, I realized what a refreshing exception Mr. Haber was to the typical golf course developer.

— Robert Muir Graves, ASGCA

During the early stages of the design process, both Edgar and Robert agreed that water elements should be designed in abundance to create and maintain the lushness of the course as not only a golfing oasis but also for all the wildfowl that lived in the dairy farm. They carefully laid out 10 separate lakes, beginning with a major lake at what would become the hotel, and then followed the elevations downward from the east bend of the Carmel River to where it winds westerly and bends back northerly at the western end of the property. In addition to their consideration for the lakes as water elements on the golf course, and for what the lakes would contribute to the overall aesthetics of the property, they laid out the lakes based on elevations so that the upper lake would drain into the next lower lake and so on. In this way they conformed to the basic topography of the land while creating the signature element of water to the golf course.

In his project log, Graves wrote in highlighted text that the "unusual features" of the golf course were 10 fresh water lakes and the Carmel River.

Muir's bid in 1960 for the golf course design, clubhouse and subdivision layout came in at $480,000. The clubhouse design included a golf shop, locker rooms, dining room, snack bar, coffee shop and cocktail lounge. Of the 245-acre footprint, the golf course used 173 acres and the subdivision used 72 acres for 166 home and condo sites. The 18-hole golf course length was laid out to be 6,756 feet from the championship tees, 6,400 feet from the men's tees and 5,471 feet and the lady's tees.

TIMELESSNESS
Quail golf course is ENDURING. Edgar was able to turn his love of golf into a business that, in turn, supported not only an elegant lifestyle but also a life of philanthropy. And he did this where he wanted to be and where it had never been done before. Quail has a quality nowhere else has. It is timeless.
— Ducky O'Toole

RARE BEAUTY
Quail is friendly to every level of player and pleasant to the eye with some spectacular views not seen on many courses, including Lincoln Park or even Cypress Point. It reflects Ed's personality: crisp, clean, open and friendly.
— Ron Reed

The golf course main characteristics were fine greens, 65 bunkers and 10 lakes. The seed selected for the greens was 100% seaside Bent Grass and the fairway seed mixture was 25% Creeping Red Fescue, 15% Chewing's Fescue, 20% Highland Bent Grass and 40% Kentucky Blue grass. The golf course construction began in June 1963 and was completed in March 1964. The first round took place in July 1964 but the grass was still young and tender, so Edgar insisted that the balls had to be teed up for all fairway shots to protect the new growth from divots.

By the time he passed in 2003, Robert Muir Graves had designed over 80 golf courses, renovated over 480 and consulted on another 200. He was a past president of the American Society of Golf Course Architects and, with Geoffrey Cornish, he co-authored the book, *Classic Golf Hole Design*.

Edgar Haber posing at the future tee of the 2nd hole.

The lake on the 17th Hole is sculpted from the natural contour of the land.

The lake on the 17th Hole when first filled with water.

The lake on the 17th Hole with landscaping becomes the "Signature Hole."

SCULPTING THE LAKES

During the 30 years since Edgar won the 1933 San Francisco Championship, he had played on most of the courses in California and neighboring states, Hawaii and Scotland, including among others the Old Course at Saint Andrews. He understood the game of golf and many of the distinctive courses on which it was played. As he carefully surveyed the topography of the pasture land in the dairy farm, he sought how best to "gently place a golf course in its natural setting." He and designer Graves agreed that the course needed a special touch, some unique course feature, something exceptional that would distinguish it from all other courses in the area, which was a particular challenge given the spectacular beauty of the oceanside courses in Pebble Beach, especially Cypress Point.

The lush river bottomland and setting beside the Carmel River inspired the idea of water as a discerning but natural feature of the land. And then it struck Edgar that a series of lakes between the fairways would not only provide challenges to the golfers but would also create an oasis-like setting for many of the fairway homes and a luscious water environment for the many types of birds he had seen in and around the old dairy farm. And by beginning the first of a series of lakes at what would become the hotel, Quail Lodge, he realized that some of the lakes would also be pleasantly visible along Valley Greens Drive.

They planned a total of 10 lakes throughout the golf course and home sites, each a different elevations so that the upper lakes could flow into the lower lakes. As a lover of wildlife and wildfowl, he knew that the lakes would preserve the habitats and provide water for deer, raccoon, coyotes, bobcats and other wild land animals as well as birds of every species, including egrets, swans, cormorants and grey herons, including migrating ducks and geese. He envisioned that the lakes would become the singular landscaping element that would distinguish Quail Lodge golf course from all others.

The excavation for the lakes was expensive and tricky. Once the entire pasture had been stripped clean of weeds and vegetation, the 18 holes were laid out. Then they could determine exactly where the lakes could be formed. Some advised him to dig the lakes 6-8 feet deep, but during the first test of digging deeply, water seeped up from the valley aquifer and Edgar knew his instinct was right to excavate shallower lakes ranging from three to four feet deep.

The lakes were gently sculpted by earth-moving equipment. When the depressions reached the desired depth, they were covered with sheets of black polyethylene to prevent water loss from seepage. A dirt berm was formed around the edges to secure the plastic sheets and prevent overflows. Pumps

were installed in each lake to aerate the water and keep it clear enough for golfers to retrieve misguided balls and clean enough for wildlife and wildfowl to quench their thirst with clear water.

Pipes that allowed water to drain from the higher elevation lakes into the lower ones connected the 10 lakes. This not only had a drain-off function, but by adding spurting water fountains, the lakes were kept aerated to prevent water stagnation that minimized algae and biofilm build up and prevented mosquitoes from breeding.

Once the lake beds were sealed and the berms in place, the lakes were filled with river water. When the lakes filled up, they accentuated the fairways and

general layout of the golf course fairways. Many years later Edgar would remark, "Installing the lakes was the single best thing we did in designing the course. Not all the golfers are happy about them when they miss a shot, you know, but the lakes as water hazards provide subtle challenges that every golfer understands and respects. And the lakes attracted so many different beautiful birds that it's hard to count them all, and they sometimes resemble a wildfowl refuge, which I like a lot. In fact, I can name every kind of duck species that lands and stays around here to rest and get a drink of water — and there are quite a few of them."

QUAIL LAKES: A WILDFOWL SANCTUARY

An articulate, if anonymous, contributor who quotes the renowned American ecologist and environmentalist Aldo Leopold (1887-1948), provided one of the most poignant descriptions of the Quail lakes as a wildfowl sanctuary. Leopold was influential in the development of environmental ethics and wildlife management and had a profound impact on the environmental movement.

The writer quotes Leopold: *"Out of the clouds I hear a faint bark, as of a faraway dog. It is strange how the world cocks its ear to that sound, wonder. Soon it is louder, the honking of geese, invisible, becoming nearer... The flock emerges from the low clouds, a banner of birds, dipping and rising, but advancing in the wind wrestling lovingly with each winnowing wing."*

The writer continues: *"Aldo Leopold knew about wild geese and wild birds of every species. As the father of scientific conservation he taught passionately about the simple needs of geese; safe and secure habitats for nesting, rearing goslings, and resting during migration. As one small but vital link in the coastal flyway, the Lakes at Quail Lodge provide an essential habitat for Canada Geese and a host of wild — and not so wild — waterfowl seeking water and a snug harbor in which to revitalize their wandering souls.*

"For the past 50-plus years Quail Lodge has voluntarily been responsible for the maintenance of the 10 lakes scattered randomly throughout the golf course. In order to preserve the lakes as a waterfowl sanctuary and to insure the tranquility of the area, access has been and will continue to be restricted to golfers, since they do not disturb the wildlife and their nesting areas.

"Residents and visitors to Quail Lodge can enjoy the seasonal arrival and departure of a growing population of geese, including the Canada Goose, and a variety of ducks. The ducks have learned how wonderfully suited Carmel Valley is for year-round living.

"Knowing your neighbors in Quail means learning to recognize Wood Ducks, Mallards, Pintail, Scaup, Buffleheads, American Wigeon, Goldeneye, Ruddy Ducks, Cinnamon Teal, Greylegs, and more. Like a few fortunate people, this banner of birds has seen a fair share of the world, wrestled with the wind, emerged from the clouds to land by choice at Quail Lodge Golf Course and call that place home."
— *Anonymous*

After the lakes were completed and the perimeters of the fairways established, which included installing an irrigation system throughout the property, the home sites were laid out. The golf course had taken up about two-thirds of the 245 acres and the remaining third became the subdivision for 150 or so home sites and two condominium clusters, which equated to about a half acre per living unit.

TEN LAKES, TEN NAMES

Edgar knew every bird by name that flew in and drank from the lakes at Quail. Once during a mid-week round I asked Edgar if he'd ever named the 10 lakes on the course. He began rattling off the names so I quickly took notes, and over time compiled the list of wildfowl names he'd given to the 10 lakes, which I don't think were ever very well known.

Ring Tail Lake, 5th green, right
Teal Lake, 5th green, back
Pintail Lake, 6th tee, front
Covey Lake, 14th fairway, left
Egret Lake, 15th fairway, left
Heron Lake, 15th green, left
Canvass Back Lake, 16th tee, right
Swan Lake, 17th tee, front, left
Hawk Lake, 18th fairway, left
Mallard Lake, Quail Lodge

And one day I recall Edgar saying, 'Well, the same birds don't always go to the same lake, which is nice because they move around a lot; besides, the lakes belong to them, you know, not us.'
— *Gary Koeppel*

But the key factor for Edgar was that the golf course came first, after which he organized the surrounding land to be used for home sites. Often developers have been known to lay out home sites in a new subdivision first and then stick in a golf course for looks and market appeal, but that wasn't what Edgar wanted to do. As it so happened, the lakes he created for the golf course as water hazards became the most desirable and therefore highest priced lots for home sites because of the increase value of any type of waterfront property.

As a resident of over 30 years I have observed thousands of birds visiting the 17th fairway lake. It's not only the prettiest lake, but it has been the "signature hole" from the day the golf course was opened in 1964. — Doris Day

In the following years as the homes were built and the landscaping evolved, the golf course and homes blended together. The fairway grasses closely bordered the neatly landscaped private yards overlooking the greens and fairways. Golfers often remarked how distinctive Quail golf course was from almost all other courses where areas of raw dirt, brown grass and weeds separated the fairways from the homes. Quail is a visually integrated residential community and golf course, which was one of the aesthetic goals of Terry Haber who oversaw all of the course landscaping that influenced the residents' homes.

Many years after the golf course had matured and the lakes were glistening with clear water that wildfowl of every species came to drink, Edgar would often take friends and guests on golf cart tours through the course, often stopping and reminiscing about a golf shot, dropping a ball and chipping to the green and putting out, or bringing attention to a particular duck's name or point out something special on the course, such as how the afternoon sun shown through the trees and dramatized the many shades of green on a hillside, all the while enjoying the natural beauty of what he always felt when he first saw the property as a beautiful dairy farm.

As the golf course and subdivision layouts were completed, as the grass seeds began to sprout on the rich soil fairways and greens, and as water began filling up the 10 lakes, Terry Haber began overseeing the golf course with course landscaper Charles Haugh and planted hundreds of trees, including cypress,

willow, fig and Japanese Peach Blossom trees, but mainly around the course perimeter she planted pine trees because of their ability to grow quickly, especially in the rich river bottom loam of the former dairy pasture. She acquired hundreds of five-gallon pots of pine trees from a Carmel Valley nursery, which were painstakingly positioned and planted throughout the property.

However, as the grasses began to take hold and mature throughout the course, at first the pine trees seemed to be taking a long time to take root and grow, and they soon lost their sheen, turned brown and died — hundreds of them.

Terry Haber was devastated. Everything else in the development was progressing smoothly and the landscaping was one of her major responsibilities. Upon investigation she discovered that the trees had been growing in their containers for an extended period of time and had become "root bound." The nursery that had sold and planted the trees had not instructed their workmen to separate the roots when removing the trees from their pots. All of the pine trees had to be dug up and replaced with new trees, the roots of which were healthy and not bound. Fortunately, because of the rich soil and careful irrigation, the new pine trees quickly took root, flourished and grew at the rate of three to five feet a year. The setback proved to be traumatic but, fortunately, temporary.

Barns Into Buildings

Never confuse your original target with the ball's final destination.

— Edgar Haber

The milk barn on the original dairy farm.

property en route to the ocean. The dairy farmer could access the eastern portion of the property only during the summer or months with low rainfall when he had to forge through the riverbed to travel from one side to the other.

Edgar needed to build a major bridge in order to connect the east and west parcels of the dairy farm. Once again, without any prior experience, but with the engineering and construction help of the county road department, he negotiated with the county to build a major bridge connecting both sides of Valley Greens Drive. After a developer creates a subdivision and installs the septic and water systems, fire hydrants and electric service, and paves the streets and walkways, the local government then assumes their ownership and maintenance.

BUILDING BRIDGES

Narrow dirt roads used by the dairy farmer for his tractors and pickups meandered throughout the dairy farm. The main dirt road, which was to become Valley Greens Drive, was connected to Carmel Valley Road on the east and San Carlos Road on the west. The Carmel River meandered throughout the property, separating the clubhouse from the lodge, and then flowed north and west of the

BUILDING HOMES

While laying out the subdivision with Jim May, his realtor and close golfing friend, Edgar and Terry went to great lengths to study the home site areas surrounding the fairways and greens. As if laying our their own home, each site was laid out individually, each with a different shaped lot, without any thought of a "grid" because they wanted each home to have its particular view of the course while also providing privacy from the adjacent property. As a result, each lot is an individual shape; no two are alike.

Construction of the bridge over the Carmel River to connect Valley Greens Drive.

The names of streets in a new development are often confusing, unrelated to the area and make no sense. The Habers wanted names that were appropriate for what was to become brand new streets in the Quail subdivision, names that were compatible with the area and everything they were building. They named the main street "Valley Greens Drive," which begins at the west entrance to the property on San Carlos Road to where it connects back to the main Carmel Valley Road. They selected other fitting names, such as Valley Greens Circle, River Place, Lake Place, and Fairway Place.

Jim May and contractors staking out the golf course home sites.

Imagine the challenge and creativity needed to organize 166 home sites in 72 acres and create an entire community of people living around a golf course — especially if you have never done that before. The exercise requires skill and sensitivity to arrange the lots individually and yet work harmoniously together as a community. As with every new challenge, together the Habers applied their fresh thinking and innate creativity to whatever came next.

Arranging the sizes, shapes and location of the lots around the golf course was an enjoyable aspect in planning the Quail residential community. Then they became involved in planning the nitty-gritty infrastructure elements, such as water lines, electric service and sewage disposal, which needed to be individual septic tanks because the larger county sewer system was not yet in service. No subdivision was allowed without streets, sidewalks, curbs, gutters, water drainage and fire hydrants. The Quail Lodge subdivision was one of the first developments in Monterey County that buried the electric power lines underground, thus preempting unsightly power poles and lines, which was another planning forethought not generally implemented in new subdivisions until years later.

For developing the plan for the home sites as well as the golf course, Edgar seemed always to take his direction from the natural lay of the land. When the course was finished, he positioned the home sites around the periphery in six different clusters. To the west, the four groups are Valley Greens Circle (the largest), River Place, Fairway Place and Valley Knoll Road; to the east, across the river, the two residential enclaves are Lake Place and Poplar Lane.

BUILDING THE CLUBHOUSE

As the consummate golfer who became the developer of a golf course, subdivision and hotel — none of which he had ever done before — Edgar knew exactly the necessary functions of a clubhouse and where it should be located. He worked closely with the architect, Charles Rose, to create the ultimate clubhouse for golfers.

During construction, before the stud walls and ceiling rafters were built, the array of stone pillars and stone fireplaces of the foundation appeared to be something of an elegant, contemporary Stonehenge.

From there the two-story structure began to take shape quickly and, as was the Habers' aesthetic intention, the roof line took on a slight Oriental look, which Edgar clarified that, "it wasn't Oriental because we didn't try to make it look Oriental, you can't fake something like that or it looks fake, but it had just a slight sense of that look, which Charlie the architect also carried through with the lodge design and, much later, with the design of our home in Quail Meadows."

Everything began and ended in the pro shop. Golfers would sign up there and end up there. It was the command and control center. Behind the shop was the workshop where clubs were fitted and repaired; behind that was the cart barn for stowing pushcarts and the new three-wheel, motored-powered carts. The

Foundation for the Quail Golf Clubhouse.

pro shop was filled with golf clubs and clothing and, in a separate room on the way to the stairway, a gift shop was located, full of unusual items, usually golf or logo oriented. In the beginning Terry selected everything for sale in the pro shop, which also included a fine line of men's and women's clothing that was not golf related. Everything selected was unique and of the highest quality. Both Edgar and Terry often said, "Good taste doesn't cost anything more" and "quality begets quality," standards by which they used for every aspect of the property they were creating.

After a round of 18 holes of golf, from the pro shop, one walked through the gift shop to the grand stairway to access the upstairs bar and lounge at the 19th hole. It was a "watering hole" not only for the golfers, but in the afternoons after work one could find members of the Quail executive staff relaxing and enjoying their beverage of choice. Why were employees allowed to drink in the country club bar? Simply put, they were not regarded as employees but instead

were treated as friends and family who worked hard and were extended almost the same privileges as members and guests.

The bar itself was a work of functional art. It extended some 50 feet long in a straight line and everyone sitting at the bar had a panoramic view overlooking the 9th fairway and green and the grassy driving range. Although popular with members and visiting golfers, as well as a few community members who knew about it, for years it remained one of the best-kept secrets in Carmel Valley.

Behind the bar were meeting rooms with floor-to-ceiling glass overlooking the wooded riverbank. Adjacent to the bar was a large function room and a smaller room that led outside. Terry Haber decorated the entire upper bar and banquet area with earth-toned carpets, tasteful wall coverings and distinctive dining tables and chairs. In order to adapt the large room for different sized functions, she created narrow, six-foot, copper-lined planter boxes on casters filled with lush plants that were easily moved around to configure the room for the desired use. It served as an elegant dining room for breakfasts and lunches overlooking the driving range in the daytime and for dinners and banquets in the evenings.

On the same level as the bar and dining room, to the east were the reception, offices and Edgar's corner office that looked the river and swimming pool. His

THE PRESIDENT AND BOARD OF DIRECTORS

OF THE

CARMEL VALLEY GOLF AND COUNTRY CLUB

REQUEST THE PLEASURE OF YOUR COMPANY

AT THE

OPENING OF OUR CLUBHOUSE

ON SATURDAY, THE FIFTH DAY OF DECEMBER

NINETEEN HUNDRED AND SIXTY-FOUR

TWO O'CLOCK UNTIL FIVE-THIRTY IN THE AFTERNOON

PLEASE PRESENT THIS INVITATION ON ARRIVAL

Lady Friday Every Day, Nancy Parsons, guarded his privacy in the outer office where she managed his schedule and member services.

A golfer and an architect who understood golfing had perfectly laid out the architecture of the clubhouse. The structure was designed to serve the functions needed by the golfer, diner and operations staff, all of which worked smoothly. Architect Charlie Rose knew how to design what Edgar wanted and where it should be placed. The interior decorator understood how to translate Terry Haber's aesthetics into an environment that was qualitative, tasteful and appealing. And so it came to be that a perfect clubhouse was created to serve the golfers, guests and members of the new Carmel Valley Golf and Country Club.

Five months after the first round of golf was played on the new course, with the greatest possible fanfare, the president and board of directors of the new Carmel Valley Golf and Country Club mailed a formal invitation to the grand opening of the Quail Golf Clubhouse to be celebrated on the fifth day of December in 1964.

Architect's rendering of Quail Lodge rooms surrounding the lakes.

BUILDING THE LODGE

As the course and clubhouse became operational, construction had already begun on the first 25 units of the hotel. The low, single-story architecture was in keeping with the lay of the land. The rooms were grouped in clusters, not rows, and the architectural lines, which conformed to the natural contours of the land, were connected by gently curved walkways. The roofs were cantilevered for both looks and rain protection. Each building cluster had flexible, inter-connecting rooms that could accommodate singles, couples, families or groups.

Framing for the first 25 Quail Lodge rooms.

People always said that Edgar makes the money and Terry spends it The interesting thing is that neither of us had never done anything like this before. As it turned out, I think we did pretty well.
— *Terry Haber*

The lodge units were situated facing the 14th fairway of the golf course. Nestled within the hotel room clusters was Mallard Lake, one of the 10 Edgar had carved into the pastures of the dairy farm. He surrounded this lake with cement block to contain the water and provide enjoyment for the guests at Quail Lodge and the fine dining restaurant, The Covey. The setting inspired Edgar to have the architect design a beautifully arched bridge across the entire lake, connecting both sides of the room clusters and making an idyllic walk for guests or a romantic setting for weddings and bridal photographs. When the hotel opened, someone donated two elegant white swans that swam gracefully around the lake for everyone's pleasure.

As Edgar explained, "We were told by the experts that the rooms had to be 422 square feet...*period*. But we said we weren't interested in that. We had traveled around and had our own ideas about being comfortable in a hotel. So we built large rooms, at least 50% larger than normal rooms at the time, so people would have more space to breathe and more comfort to enjoy. We wanted what we wanted — not necessarily because it hadn't been done before — and we just were not interested in how it was done by someone somewhere else."

Architect's rendering of Quail Lodge.

Early development of Quail Lodge.

View of the arched bridge from a finished room.

He continued, "Another thing, for example, we didn't want a typical bathroom. We wanted a space where ladies could sit down in a private area in front of a mirror to put on their makeup, and a large bath tub for women and a shower for men with a large shower head. And we wanted some cottages where a large family or a golf foursome could stay with four separate bedrooms all connected to a fifth room which was the common living room for entertaining."

Regarding the Quail Lodge interiors, Terry Haber said, "I always represented Edgar and what he wanted when working with the architect, landscaper or interior designer. When we got to selecting furniture, fabrics or anything visible, although I was responsible to bring it all off, I was always able to read what Edgar wanted: the colors, styles, earth tones, real wood, whatever it was, but it was always quality. We argued back and forth about the costs of this or that, but he insisted on quality, which is what I chose, and in the end he always opted for the best and so that's what we did, always quality, often whether we could afford it or not."

Architect's rendering of interior of Quail Lodge lobby.

PRIVATE OR PUBLIC GOLF COURSE?

As we were putting the golf course together and, at the same time, laying out the lots and developing plans for the clubhouse, we had a lot of discussions about the advantages and disadvantages between a public golf course and a private club. A public golf course didn't fit into the level of quality we wanted for the entire operation but an equity membership club was out of the question, too, because we had investors who were the basic owners. I had traveled around quite a bit and played a lot of tournaments at a lot difference types of golf courses, mostly in California but some outside, including Hawaii, so I kinda knew what worked. The clubs that were successful had hotels, which is where the main source of money comes from, so we needed rooms as part of the package. Most clubs I knew had 400 or so members, but then guests would not be able to play golf there until, say, after 10 in the morning so we kept our membership down to around 200, which turned out to be manageable for everyone. That way we didn't have to encourage a lot of otherwise outside, or public play, but I wrote letters to a lot of clubs inviting their members to play here and arranged some reciprocal play, so that worked out well even for our members who could play for reduced rates at other clubs. We decided to name the place The Carmel Valley Golf and Country Club and kept that name for years until the Carmel Valley Ranch was developed and caused a lot of name confusion, so we changed the name to Quail Lodge Resort and Golf Club. So, we liked the name and everyone was happy.

— Edgar Haber

Washed Out, Not Washed Up

When I blew up the cart bridge between 11 & 12 to stop the river from flooding the golf course and homes, we were washed out, but not washed up.

— Edgar Haber

As the lodge was being completed and Terry was busy with the decorator selecting carpets, paints, furniture, bedding, towels and everything else, the Habers knew a hotelier that had managed a motel Edgar had built on Munras Avenue in Monterey, the King's Lodge. He was a very proper British gentleman by the name of Les Knapton who became the start up manager of the hotel as it was being constructed.

Mr. Knapton, as he preferred to be called by everyone, including the Habers, brought his English eloquence, etiquette and excellence to Carmel Valley, where farmers still sold their fruits and vegetables in rustic stands along Carmel Valley Road, and where cowboys and ranchers still drove their dusty pickups with rifles hanging across racks in the back window.

IN THE PRESENCE OF THE QUEEN

As kids, my sister Marilyn, brother Warren and I were scared to death of Mr. Knapton because he was so British, all formal and proper, you'd think you were in the presence of the Queen of England. But one time during Halloween when my sister was in high school, she got caught throwing the stinky rotten eggs on Ocean Avenue in Carmel. Marilyn was the angel of the family and never created waves or did anything wrong. My mom was out of town and dad was in a meeting, and she's sitting in the police station completely terrified about what was going to happen to her, so then Mr. Knapton arrives in his three-piece suite, all proper like, right into the Carmel Police Station as if he owned it, to fetch her and take her home. She was scared as could be, but all he said was, 'Oh well, jolly good, no harm, no foul, let's go home.'

— Anne Haber

Edgar recalled his English gentleman start up manager. "Mr. Knapton was meticulous and fussy about everything at the lodge, from how to fold napkins and towels; how to 'dress' a roll of toilet paper by folding down the edge; yes, even how to turn a lamp so that the seam of the shade was not visible. All of the rooms had to have a brewer and their own coffee and teas, English tea, of course, and in the afternoons the bedspread was turned down and special chocolates were put on the pillow for the guests. Every day he had staff place fresh flowers in a clean vase in each room. Details, he was as possessed by details as we were, which is partly how Quail Lodge was soon to become a Five-Star Mobil Resort."

Edgar continued, "In addition to bringing his knowledge of first-class taste, service and amenities to the hotel, Mr. Knapton was also a stickler for his own privacy. He occupied one of the 25 rooms in the first phase of the hotel development, a room that nobody, including me, was ever allowed to enter because he said, 'This is my house,' so we respected his privacy. And he taught the staff how to respect a guest's privacy by never, that is, never ever enter a guest room without first knocking in a certain soft way and announcing room service, housekeeping or security, then waiting patiently for a response."

Edgar explained the uniforms worn by the Quail Lodge bell men. "They had shined shoes, dark slacks and a tan, hunting-style jacket with a thick outside belt on which hung a Motorola radio. Not only was the radio helpful to communicate important messages between staff, it provided immediate communication with the front desk, or room service or engineering about a guest's need or problem, which expedited prompt service. But the uniform also resembled a security uniform conveying some kind of law enforcement, especially because the Motorola radio on the belt strapped outside their jacket made them look pretty official. We didn't have any security staff and didn't need any because all the bell man looked like security officers and were trained to act appropriately during an emergency."

Arnold Palmer on the practice range.

Edgar always credited the game of golf to be the source for everything good that ever happened to him during his life, for which there are many examples throughout this book. For one example, one day during his early years when freshening up in the locker room of a San Francisco golf course, a man asked him what he did for a living, to which Edgar replied that he was currently without work. After sizing him up, the man gave him his card and told him if he ever wanted a job to give him a call. Edgar never called him but always remembered how a door had been opened.

Another prominent gentleman came to the lodge asking for accommodations — not in the hotel, but for an extended period, so Edgar arranged for him to stay in the Quail condominium of a friend who was on vacation. Two years later he saw the same guest practicing on the putting green with a horrible looking putter and asked him what kind of terrible accident had befallen the club. Somewhat taken aback, the guest replied that the putter had a sentimental value because a friend named Arnold Palmer given it to him.

Edgar was delighted to hear that and told him that Arnold was a mutual friend who often stayed at Quail Lodge when playing tournaments in Pebble Beach. The man replied, "Yes, I know. Arnold asked me for a good place to stay that was away from the hustle and bustle of Pebble Beach and I told him to come here." The man was Walter Scott, chairman of the board of NBC and on the board of RCA and other major corporations, who was also a member of the Cypress Point Club. Edgar and Walter Scott became close friends over the years and Edgar was always astonished that one never knew whom you were going to meet on a golf course.

A golfer drives on the 10th tee of the new course.

FIRST DAY, FIRST TEE, FIRST DRIVE, FIRST DIVOT

I first met Edgar when I was in high school with Marilyn. When he opened the golf course in 1964 he generously offered the course to the Carmel High School golf team, which I was on. And a very memorable day, he pre-opened the golf course and allowed the team to come and play but, because the grass was so young, we were required to hit every shot off the fairway with a tee because he didn't want you to take divots and that gave the grass time to mature. And, always one to take full advantage of the moment, he had The Herald *out to take pictures to promote the high school team and also the opening day of the Quail golf course. A fairly large gallery had gathered around the first tee with photographer and guests and staff. I think I'm a junior in high school and as I get up on the tee getting ready to hit, I get a little nervous and I fired a little bit early with my driver and took a huge divot right there in front of Edgar and everyone, which was a cringing occurrence for him because the divot happened on the first day of play on the first tee on the new grass of the beautiful new Carmel Valley Golf and Country Club by a high school golfer who should never take a divot. Inside he's going nuts but, seizing the moment, he takes the opportunity to demonstrate to the rest of the high school team players the proper way to replace a divot. So that's how that began. That was my first meeting with Edgar Haber. At the same time, it was both mortifying and hilarious.*

— Lawson Little

THE BET FOR FIVE

Before tournaments Arnold Palmer practiced at Quail. One day he asked Edgar if he would like to play 18 holes. Edgar was ecstatic. Imagine, playing a private round of golf with Arnold Palmer! He was a little nervous as he warmed up on the first tee but as Arnold stepped up to drive he said, "Edgar, let's have a little bet on the game, say, five?" Edgar said, "Sure." But as he hit his first drive, it occurred to him he wasn't sure what Arnold had meant by "five." As he walked down the first fairway, he began to fret in earnest. Did Arnold mean five dollars or five hundred? Or, given Arnold's status and success, could he have meant five thousand?

As Edgar played each hole — as always to the best of his ability, which was impressive as a semi-professional amateur — the amount of the bet continued to gnaw at him but he couldn't bring himself to ask Arnold how much. The match went back and forth, but never a shot or two difference between them. By the time they reached the 18th green, Edgar was one stroke down. Arnold's chip shot landed about nine feet from the hole whereas Edgar's ball was nearly 20 feet away. He knew a two-putt would cost him the hole — and the match — and then who knows how much he'd need to cough up to honor the bet. With rattled nerves Edgar focused hard and holed his putt for a birdie. Arnold finished with a par and the match was tied. Although slightly disappointed that he didn't win, he was greatly relieved with a tie, and still felt awkward to ask about the bet. He never did find out whether Arnold's "five" was for dollars, hundreds or thousands but he finally became content with never knowing.

Edgar Haber putting to tie Arnold Palmer on the 18th,

BLOWING BRIDGES

Although the Monterey County Road Department built the bridge on Valley Greens Drive that spanned the east and west parcels of the old dairy farm and connected the Golf Clubhouse with Quail Lodge, there were two areas where the river meandered through the new golf course that needed to be connected by a foot and cart bridge for the golfers.

Edgar watching the flood waters eroding the 11th fairway.

Bridges were needed between the fairway and the green at the 6th hole and between the green at the 11th and tee box at the 12th. At considerable but necessary expense, Edgar built two slightly arched concrete bridges that essentially completed the golf course.

During the winter of 1969 heavy rains flooded the Carmel River and brought tons of mud, boulders and entire trees swirling downstream. The debris was so dense and violent that it piled up against the footings and cement walkway of the bridge. The debris quickly piled up against the bridge and created a dam that diverted the floodwaters out of its banks and surged into the 11th and 12th fairways, eroding hundreds of yards of the golf course.

The greens crew and many Quail employees filled and placed sandbags from 5:00 in the morning until 11:00 at night, then others came in and worked with huge spotlights through the night, but the river kept rising and eroding more and more land. Edgar stood helpless, watching his dream golf course being washed away. When the diverted river began to erode the land where the maintenance shed is now located at the 13th green, Edgar realized he had to blow the bridge to divert the river's flow. He called a fellow golfer and friend, the Army Commandant at Fort Ord, who soon arrived with a squad of men and packages of explosives.

FLOODED WITH LOYALTY

When the river flooded, the power went out, it was miserable and we had guests in the hotel. Almost every off-duty employee voluntarily came and worked to help out, including barbecuing food outdoors for the guests, filling sand bags in the rain and doing whatever was needed to get through it. They did it out of loyalty to the Habers.

— Mary Bayless

Inspecting the debris build-up against the damaged cart bridge.

As the Army demolition experts shimmied out on cables over the raging river and placed the dynamite charges on the bridge, A solder wired the detonator box and brought it to the commandant to blow, but he did not have the heart for it and said to his friend Edgar, "Okay, I've set it, but I don't have the heart for it so I'm not going to blow it. It's all yours." He handed the detonator to Edgar who, pausing briefly, took a deep breath and pressed the plunger. The cement bridge exploded into thousands of pieces releasing tons of backed up debris that quickly began flowing downstream, retuning the river to its channel and preventing further damage to the golf course and homes downstream.

The flood was devastating to Edgar's spirit as he saw a part of his golf course washed away; the winter rains had also played havoc with tourism in general

The flood was the most upsetting experience in Edgar's life. It was around 1969 during one of the Crosby Clambake affairs, and we had just completed getting the hotel and everything opened and running smoothly. Cash flow was tough and we were selling lots in the subdivision at low prices just to pay bills and make payroll. The river kept taking more and more of the golf course and all we could do is stand there and watch it happen. It was as if all our dreams were washing down the river. It's sad to see a grown man cry, but that's what he did, for a few moments anyway, and then he picked himself up and forged ahead, blew the bridge and began putting the place back together.
— Terry Haber

and with Quail Lodge specifically because it had just gotten everything open for business and was almost immediately shut down. Not only were the Habers stunned with the unexpectedness, speed and extent of the reversal, the well-trained and highly motivated staff was suddenly confronted with the possibility of losing their jobs. It took only one day after the blowing of the bridge for the Habers to call a general meeting of all employees, and when everyone gathered in the banquet room they were prepared for the worst possible news. Instead, their fears were relieved and their hopes revived.

The flooding damaged more than the bridge and golf course; the havoc it wreaked also damaged business and created some serious cash flow problems for the business. The Habers had never missed a payroll nor had ever been late with payments to a vendor invoice or the bank mortgage. But this time Edgar had no choice but to request the bank to extend him the courtesy of a few deferred payments. He called and made what he hoped would not be his last meeting with the bank, but as a realist he knew it was at best a 50-50 chance the bank would refuse his request for even minor restructuring.

THINGS WILL GET BETTER

Right after the flood and the bridge was blown,
the Habers called in all 225 employees, and
Mr. Haber said, 'I just want you to know, we're
family…and nobody is going to lose their job.
We are going to weather through this together.
Everybody is going to help each other. We are all
safe and very soon everything will get better.'
You could hear the sigh of relief in the room
and feel the quiet love for this man.

— Jeanie Gould

Removing debris to restore the flow of water.

CONGRATULATIONS, YOU NOW OWN A GOLF COURSE

During the meeting to negotiate a minor loan modification, after Edgar presented the board members with his proposals and projections
for recovering from the flood, with very little discussion, the bank politely but promptly declined his request. After a minute, Edgar stood up and
said, 'All right, gentlemen, congratulations, you now own a golf course,' and then promptly walked from the room out of the bank to his car.
He told me later that as he was driving away, he was shaking as he wondered if he'd done the right thing by bluffing, doubting himself
and everything else, and then he heard, 'Ed, Ed, Ed… come back here and let's talk,' said one of the Bank's board members as he ran
toward Edgar's car. Fifteen minutes later the bank agreed to give him a two-year extension, interest free, which gave him all the time he
needed to rebuild after the flood. And he still never missed a payroll.

— Steve Gould

Five Cheers For Five Stars

Good taste doesn't cost anything and excellence doesn't cost much more, but neither are negotiable.

— Edgar Haber

The first official General Manager of Quail Lodge was a Hungarian hotelier named Csaba Ajan (pronounced chubba a-jan) who had studied hospitality at San Diego State College and had first worked in the lavish Hotel del Coronado and was then hired as the food and beverage manager for the landmark Hotel El Cortez. He took a trip to Carmel and made a courtesy visit to the then general manager of the Lodge at Pebble Beach, Tom Oliver, who a few weeks later, phoned Csaba and said a fellow in Carmel Valley has a golf club and is building a new hotel for which he is looking for a general manager.

When Csaba visited the property a few weeks later, he met the British gentleman Edgar had brought out of retirement to help with the hotel start up details, Les Knapton, who Csaba recollects as a "very conservative, proper English gentleman who looked like the UK's prime minister, Anthony Eden, mustache, manners and all. Then when I met Edgar and Terry Haber, I knew the property had the potential to be a great one."

While negotiating with the Habers for the general manager position, Csaba coincidentally received a bona fide offer to become the food and beverage manager of the Century Plaza Hotel in Los Angeles, one of the most prestigious hotel properties in the country where every major foreign dignitary stayed when visiting the west coast. A few weeks later Csaba chose Quail Lodge, that was, in his words, "a new hotel still under construction, located in a remote rural area and situated beside the organically fertilized lettuce fields of a third generation farmer."

It was a daring decision by Csaba because on the Monterey Peninsula if you are not in Pebble Beach, Pacific Grove, Monterey or the Highlands, you are simply not on the ocean; you are in a valley.

Csaba turned down the Plaza and opted for Quail because it was not only unopened and untested, which was challenging, to say the least, but he surmised that Edgar and Terry Haber were fascinating people who knew how to get

1980 Mobil 5-Star Award winners

things done and, more importantly, how to get them done the right way. Csaba had learned the land Haber bought was zoned for 240 or more tract homes, but instead of maximizing his investment with a full build out, the Habers opted for quality. They had built a first-class golf course, then wisely asked the county for a zoning variance, but not before he dedicated the golf course to be forever preserved as "greenbelt" where nothing could be built in the future, which then allowed fewer homes to be built but also on smaller lots of land. In short, Csaba was impressed.

As the golf course matured and the hotel was completed, what made Quail Lodge special? As Csaba explained, "Well, the rooms were not only brand new but twice the size of almost all other hotels and their décor was stunning. Mr. Haber's wife, Terry, was a master of good taste and design: she hired the famous lifestyle restaurant and furniture designer from San Francisco, McGuire, who provided the lodge with high-end, timeless, Rolls Royce quality Rattan furniture. Terry complemented the furniture by decorating every room individually with different furniture pieces, styles and colors, which used to challenge the housekeeping staff but created endless compliments from the guests."

Csaba related a humorous story about their major but friendly competitor, the Del Monte Lodge, now called The Lodge at Pebble Beach, that traditionally ran full-page advertisements in *Sunset Magazine* promoting their golf package with the caveat, in a bold-letter headline: "In Case of Inclement Weather, Your Green Fees Will Be Credited."

Although not a golfer, after reading the Pebble Beach ad, Csaba came up with a mischievous idea to run Quail's golf package advertisement on the adjacent page with the same size ad that read: *"At Quail Lodge Golf Course every day is sunny and we never need to refund green fees to anyone."* Edgar and even the folks at Pebble Beach got quite a kick over the ad that, not surprisingly, brought in a lot of smiles and play to the course from out-of-town golfers.

By 1973 all of the 100 rooms at the lodge as well as The Covey restaurant had been opened and were operating splendidly. All systems were fully operational,

the now seasoned staff had matured and guest services were considered exemplary. Everything had evolved better than anyone could have ever imagined. Membership in the Carmel Valley Golf and Country Club had reached 200 and morale was high throughout the Quail community of residents, members, guests and staff. The golf course was full of play by members, by lodge guests and by visiting members of other country clubs throughout the country.

VIP professional golfers, such as Arnold Palmer, Jack Nicklaus and Gary Player were frequent guests of the lodge while playing in the major tournaments in Pebble Beach. Prominent presidents and CEOs of major corporations enjoyed the casual elegance of Quail Lodge, dining in its superb restaurant and golfing on a first-class course that could be played almost every day of the year. All of the condominium units and residential lots had been sold and lovely homes with lush landscaping surrounded the golf course fairways and lakes.

The Covey Restaurant quickly developed a reputation of excellence for both food and décor. The restaurant was designed to be in the center of the lodge with units on both sides with all of the seating facing Mallard Lake with a fountain in the middle and an oriental arched walking bridge separating it from the 14th fairway. Two white swans were the permanent residents of the lake and ducks of every kind and color swam everywhere. The Covey interior was as elegant inside as it was outside and featured unusual objects that were often indistinguishable but always appropriate and were sparsely but aesthetically placed throughout the bar and restaurant.

Quail had an exceptional team of employees. During the 1970s there were many labor disputes in hotels throughout the Monterey Peninsula, but there was never a dispute or union strike at Quail Lodge. Why not? Csaba explained, "We had the good fortune of working with professional owners with kind hearts and integrity and with an exceptionally good staff who were not only treated like family by the Habers but who also acted like family; they took pride in their work and did whatever needed doing. We had a great but lean staff. Everyone was cross-trained; a sommelier could wait tables, a waiter could sell wine, a hostess could serve and a sales person could step into the front desk. Everyone worked together, literally as a family, and that's what made everything else work well."

As but one measure of the growing reputation of what was originally known as the Carmel Valley Golf and Country Club, on January 17, 1969 SFB Morse, the

S. F. B. MORSE
PEBBLE BEACH
CALIFORNIA

January 17, 1969

My dear Ed:

Thank you very much for the complimentary cards to the club. I have long wanted to take Mrs. Morse there, but have hesitated a little bit because I haven't been a member. We shall go there soon.

I hope you are having continued success. I hear highly of the course and the entire operation.

Very sincerely,

Mr. Edgar H. Haber
President
Carmel Valley Golf and Country Club
Route 2, Box 2300
Carmel, California

The Covey restaurant interior décor was Terry's piece de resistance. The objects were unusual, such as an antique grain rack, a Moroccan chandelier full of color, an antique spinning wheel — unusual objects that people could not readily recognize but enjoyed their inherent beauty.
— Carmen Ajan

founder of the Pebble Beach Company, wrote a letter to Edgar thanking him for a complimentary membership and expressing his regret for not bringing Mrs. Morse to Quail Lodge sooner. In closing, he wrote, "I hear highly of the course and the entire operation." If a new hotelier desired an endorsement from anyone in the world, a compliment from the legendary SFB Morse was incomparable.

Then in 1975 the General Manager, Csaba Ajan, received a telegram that read:

CONGRATULATIONS. STOP. QUAIL LODGE HAS WON
THE MOBIL FIVE-STAR AWARD. STOP. DETAILS TO FOLLOW. STOP.

At first Csaba thought the telegram might be a prank because humor was not in short supply throughout the Quail world of members, guests, friends and family, where someone was always pulling off some kind of good-natured trick on someone else. So to make sure he wasn't the brunt of a joke, Csaba telephoned the *Mobil Travel Guide* Awards Department in the offices of the publisher, Rand McNally. He finally reached the man in charge of the awards who confirmed the telegram and offered his enthusiastic congratulations. Csaba was flabbergasted.

Csaba recalled, "Prior to that time, Quail Lodge's highest award was the second highest Triple A Travel Award for Northern California. But a Five-Star Mobil Award? It was the highest possible award in the entire hospitality industry. It's what an Academy Award is to the movie industry. When considering a hotel property for the award, the anonymous Five-Star inspector had a checklist of over 250 items on which high scores were needed just to be qualified. Established hotels, such as the Santa Barbara Biltmore, or even the Hotel Del Coronado, had never received a Five-Star Award. And, yet, here it was, the ultimate recognition of excellence for Carmel Valley Golf and Country Club in Carmel Valley, California!" Then Csaba recalled his first impressions of Quail Lodge in a dusty valley filled with cows and crops, cowboys and farmers, tractors and pick ups. Remotely located or not, quality is quality and excellence begets excellence.

The Habers and the entire staff were ecstatic and the excellence of their collaborative efforts would continue to be awarded with Five Stars for many years to come. Over the next 20 years, Quail Lodge received this most-prestigious award 20 times — far more than any other property in the history of the award anywhere in the United States. The announcement of the winners of the 1980 award, Quail's fifth of 20, illustrated the prestige and level of

Edgar Haber receives Mobil 5-Star Award.

Quail Lodge gets five-star rating for 20th year

BY ALEX HULANICKI
Herald Staff Writer

When Quail Lodge opened in 1963, Ed Haber relied on invitations to golf pros and members of private golf clubs to market the dairy-turned-resort in Carmel Valley.

Now, Haber lets Mobil Travel Guides tout the resort, which this week was awarded a five-star rating for the 20th year.

Quail Lodge is one of only four resorts in California, five on the West Coast and 23 in the country to receive Mobil's coveted ranking.

"It's the most respected quality recognition in our industry," said Csaba Ajan, vice president and managing director at Quail Lodge. "It's like the Academy Awards every year."

Maintaining the five-star status is more crucial than obtaining it, Haber said yesterday. Falling a rung on the ladder, he said, results in bigger headlines than achieving status quo.

This week, four California resorts lost one of their five stars. They are the Four Seasons Hotel at Beverly Hills, the Hotel Bel Air in Los Angeles and the Four Seasons Clift and the Stouffer Stanford

Court, both in San Francisco.

In addition to Quail Lodge, the California resorts still in the highest Mobil stratosphere are the Ritz Carlton in Laguna Niguel, The Peninsula in Beverly Hills and the Ritz Carlton in San Francisco.

"Consistency of service, continued upkeep and impeccable housekeeping are the key ingredients to maintaining a five-star rating," according to criteria published by Mobil.

Haber said that Mobil's inspectors surreptitiously visit five-star properties several times a year to make sure that the property is worthy of the rating.

From the initial telephone call for a reservation to a welcome gift from management, the property must measure up to Mobil's standards, Haber said.

Quail Lodge first achieved five-star status in 1974 and held it for nine years. Then, the 800-acre resort lost a star for two years before regaining its previous status.

Haber and his partners, who now number 65, started out with no experience in running a hotel, golf course and residential development. But, he said, he depended on the expertise of a local architect, Charles Rose, landscaper, Chuck Haugh, and

See FIVE-STAR RATING PAGE 2C

Ed Haber stands on the deck outside the Quail Lodge golf clubhouse yesterday.
Robert Fish/The Herald

excellence associated with Mobil Five Star Awards. The award-winning hotels for that year were the Beverly Wilshire Hotel, the Four Seasons-Clift Hotel, Stanford Court and…Quail Lodge Resort.

Through the next few years, the Five-Star Award continued to be bestowed on the property for its excellence on every level of quality and service, getting high grades for the 250-item list that was checked off every year when the Mobil official arrived for his annual inspection. The anonymous inspector always visited using an assumed name. Mobil never announced when the inspector would visit so that the property had no time to prepare and was graded on their normal, every day performances. However, one year, Edgar got lucky when a friend in public relations coincidentally met the Mobil Five-Star inspector and sent her photo to Edgar, who posted it at the front desk.

As the years passed and the awards kept coming, so also increased the number and difficulty of the requirements necessary to obtain the award, and so it became more and more challenging to maintain the five-star status. Edgar became known for creating increasingly challenging tasks for the staff to perform in order to continue polishing their now stellar reputation, which is how the bizarre catering event evolved that required renting a helicopter to serve a five-star dinner on a remote beach in southern California no fewer that 200 miles south of Quail Lodge:

THE FIVE-STAR CATERING CAPER

At one of the Mobil Five-Star Award dinners, the cute, young event-production lady told Edgar they would soon be shooting a commercial somewhere near Carmel and, as was just like Ed, he said, 'Great, here's my card. Give me a call and if it's close to Carmel, we'll cater dinner for you.' Several months later, one day in the early afternoon, the cute young events lady phoned Edgar and asked sweetly, 'Mr. Haber, remember that little thing you said about catering dinner for us?' 'Oh, yes,' he replied, 'so where are you?' She said they were shooting a film on the beach near Santa Maria, which is about 200 miles south of Quail Lodge in Carmel Valley. Edgar was grateful he had a good team to pull off his ill-fated promise and they all sprang into action. We had a really great team who immediately began to pull everything together, Csaba the GM, Rob Wheat the controller, Bob Williamson the chef and Mike Patterson the club manager. But they didn't just slam together box lunches, no that wasn't a Five-Star effort. Instead, they packed the finest China and silverware, silver candelabras and an amazing array of food dishes and several cases of wines, champagnes and fine Cognacs. Csaba found a small plane and we flew everything down to the Santa Maria airport where the film crew's two-person helicopter shuttled everything down to some sand dunes on a remote beach. I recall the chef cooking the prepped food on a Coleman stove on the beach and we served a five-course dinner on linen-covered folding tables. It was a production to best all productions. It was Five Star. It was Haber. The catered event became famous among Five-Star properties and our reputation knew no bounds, but I think after that Mr. Haber became more careful about extending catering invitations to cute little event production gals.

— Steve Gould

THE HELICOPTER STORY

Arnold Palmer preferred staying in the valley quietude of Quail Lodge to avoid the crowds of fans at Pebble Beach during the Crosby Clambake and US Open Golf Tournaments. Edgar recalled how Arnold Palmer came to be a repeat guest at Quail Lodge during the tournaments:

"A friend called up one day and he said, 'I understand that you have a new place down there and Arnold Palmer would like three rooms for the Crosby Tournament.' So when he said that, I'm thinking, three rooms, eh? And we only had 25 rooms, so that's more than 10% of our room capacity, especially during the Crosby when every room in the area is 100% booked. And I knew it was customary not

to charge big shots, so when I hesitated, the voice said, 'Well, would you like a deposit?' He was smarter than I was, and I said, 'Well, yeah, because we're just kind of scraping by.' And he says, 'Fine.'

"So, Arnold Palmer arrives and we charge him for three rooms, which was a little embarrassing at first, but after while, I found out he liked that because he didn't have to go to cocktail parties or anything, he just paid for his room and that was that, whereas everybody else gives him everything for nothing except that he's got to show up for the ladies tea and this and that."

During the first Crosby tournament while staying at Quail Lodge, Arnold got caught in traffic driving between Quail Lodge and Pebble Beach. He arrived a

The helicopter that became famous for flying professional golfers from Quail Lodge to tournaments in Pebble Beach.

few minutes late for his tee time and the officials charged him a two-stroke penalty. As a fellow golfer and friend, Edgar felt terrible about the penalty and somewhat responsible because he was Arnold's Innkeeper.

So when the 1972 US Open was approaching, Edgar was hoping that Arnold would return to Quail after the two-stroke penalty incident, but also not wanting him to suffer another penalty if he got caught in traffic again between Quail and Pebble. One day he confided his concern to his old friend, Hank Ketchem, the cartoonist of Dennis the Menace comic strip, who said simply, "So, why don't you get a helicopter?"

When Edgar learned a helicopter rented for about $600 an hour plus pilot, lodging and fuel expenses, he figured that a helicopter was out of the question. But always the optimist, Edgar telephoned the nearest office of Bell Helicopter in Van Nuys, and asked to speak with the president, whose secretary asked to know what he wanted to discuss with him, to which Edgar replied, "Well, if he plays golf, he'll understand; if he doesn't, well, then never mind." She said, "Oh, he plays golf, just a minute."

Edgar Haber with a helicopter outside the clubhouse.

So the voice on the phone asked what he wanted, and Edgar said, "Well, we're going to have the US Open here this year and Arnold Palmer, Gary Player and some other golfers are staying here, and we need to get them from Carmel Valley to Pebble Beach without them being late and getting penalized. They would be flying in your helicopter every day from Quail Lodge to Pebble Beach and, you know, the national newspapers are going to ask where they're staying and what helicopter they're riding in, which all sounds like a tremendous amount of free publicity nationwide, but we can't afford to rent us."

The voice at the other end immediately said, "Okay, I get it. Sure. Okay, I can send you a five-seat bird for a week but I need a room for the pilot and you pay the fuel and insurance," then all matter-of-fact like, he hung up. So for the entire week of the Open we ferried the players and friends back and forth from Quail to Pebble. My friend at the *San Francisco Chronicle,* Art Rosenbaum, ran a piece with the headline: *To the First Tee by Helicopter.* No one had every done that before so it was news. The story ran with photos of Arnold and the Helicopter in 600 syndicated national newspapers. It got extensive TV and radio coverage all over. Quail Lodge and Bell Helicopter received a lot of national exposure and publicity — and it only cost a room, some food and a bunch of fuel.

Edgar was excited about the success of the helicopter. The media had loved it almost as much as the players. When the tournament was over and the helicopter flew back to its base, Edgar telephoned the president of Bell Helicopter and said, "I am calling to thank you for the use of your helicopter. Everyone thought it was a great idea, all the golfers made their tee times and we got national publicity for our hotel and your helicopter. I just wanted to thank you personally." There was a long pause at the other end of the line, and then the president asked briskly, "What helicopter? Who the hell gave you a helicopter?"

Edgar never knew what happened to the executive who authorized the helicopter, but he hoped the president had a sense of humor and wrote him a letter inviting him to Quail for a stay and a round of golf.

When A Covey Is A Family

If you can't say something nice to someone, it's best not to say anything.

— Edgar Haber

QUALITY, HOSPITALITY AND KINDNESS

It is remarkable that a golfer and a schoolteacher would be able to convert a rural dairy farm into an elegant five-star resort. With no previous experience, they created a golf course and clubhouse, subdivision, hotel and country club. But they had unseen talents that permeated everything they touched: an unswerving commitment to quality, an uncanny understanding of hospitality and an innate kindness in all manners of treatment of their employees. These three distinctive attributes, quality, hospitality and kindness, were the foundations of their success.

Other than Terry Haber, Lawson Little is perhaps the most knowledgeable living person about the history of Quail Lodge and the reasons for its success. As its former president, only recently retired, Lawson worked 36 years for Quail Lodge, first in the golf shop overseeing the golf cart fleet, then as the Habers' close assistant and confidant, overseeing the planning, development and sales of Quail Meadows, and finally as the president of the company after Edgar passed.

Lawson Little (left) with Edgar Haber.

MONEY CAN'T BUY IT

Because of an atmosphere of friendliness and kindness to each other and guests, Quail employees enjoyed coming to work… each employee felt so proud that they worked at Quail…and that feeling was transmitted throughout property, which created a wonderful environment of relaxed genuine friendliness to each and every guest. Every good hotel has good rooms and good beds. But not every hotel has a relaxed, warm and friendly feel. Quail's wonderful environment was most definitely motivated by leadership and by the understanding that these feelings come from integrity, grace and elegance, which were exampled by Terry and Edgar Haber, something money simply cannot buy.
— Lawson Little

Lawson's father, Lawson Little was the greatest match player in the history of golf…and to this day remains the only player to have won both the British and US Amateur Championships in the same year — more than once. As a professional, he won eight tournaments including the 1940 United States Open and is also an inductee into the World Golf Hall of Fame. Lawson grew up in an environment of renowned golfers and athletes and is no stranger to greatness, a quality that probably attracted him to work for Edgar and Terry Haber for nearly four decades.

Perhaps Lawson's greatest achievement as Edgar Haber's right arm was his role in the development of Quail Meadows, the Habers' second subdivision after the golf estates. The 614-acre, 56-lot subdivision required 14 years of planning and development to complete, in part because there were 104 environmental conditions that had to be met before the development could begin.

Quail Meadows gated community subdivision was created from a portion of the Fish Ranch overlooking the entrance to Carmel Valley and the Pacific Ocean

EMPLOYEES ARE FAMILY

Terry Haber's true calling was her ability to hire the right people for the right role for the golf course, clubhouse and hotel operations. She personally hired every employee, several hundred of them over time. Once a new person was hired, their first duty was to meet 'Mr. Haber,' as he was always respectfully called, and he would always take time to talk with them before they officially began work.

The Habers believed that although they could create a quality environment, in order for the property to be successful it had to imbue all of the intangible qualities of hospitality, which meant that the people *ARE* the place, an insight they somehow intuited and always implemented.

Another quality they imbued and practiced with their "employee family members" was their ability to teach by example and to lead gracefully, another characteristic that garnered their employees' professional respect and personal affection.

A strong part of Terry's talent was her feeling for the people she hired and her thoughtful treatment of them. She knew each one of the 250 employees by name, the name of their spouse and the names of all their children. The entire families were invited to the annual employee Christmas parties and Terry made certain that not only did everyone receive a gift, but that each child received an appropriate gift based on their sex and age, complete with their personal name on the gift tag.

One of the remarkable accomplishments of the Habers was the loyalty they were able to cultivate in their employees, not by design but simply by the way they treated the people who worked for them. At the peak of Quail's success as a Mobil Five-Star resort property, over 250 employees were on payroll. But despite the numbers, the Habers never treated employees as employees, but rather as members of their extended family.

Many employees have expressed their appreciation for the treatment given them by the Habers that, in turn, made it easy for the employees to be loyal. This loyalty was put to the test during the 1973-75 recession, which followed the major flood event that eroded the golf course and flooded several homes. The recession nearly brought businesses throughout the Monterey Peninsula to a halt. With the lodge at near zero occupancy and still recovering from the devastating flood a few years earlier, with cash flow reduced to a cash trickle,

FELIZ NAVIDAD

The Habers were extremely generous with employees.
Every year in December one of the Mexican greens keepers
would take his family to Mexico and miss the annual
Christmas Party, so Terry would buy and wrap gifts for the
entire family that they opened on their drive to Mexico.
— Mary Bayless

THE JOB INTERVIEW

The day I applied to work at Quail Lodge, as I parked, Mr. Haber
drove up in his little Mercedes. Although he was wearing a
beautiful suit, he stooped down and picked up a cigarette butt,
then looked around for anything else littering the parking lot.
During the interview he asked why I wanted to work there.
I replied that I had seen him picking up cigarette butts in the
parking lot and saw his personal pride of the property. I said
I wanted to work there because it was such a beautiful place that
I would take care of it the same way he did. And I got the job.
— Sidney Reade

FAMILY

Family comes from love, from caring and from commitment.
Ed and Terry Haber's Quail Lodge was loyal to its clientele,
to its members and especially to its employees. The loyalty was
reciprocal and rather incredible in every relationship. How
incredible? Simple. Just imagine the amount of love, care and
loyalty it took for employees to remain working here for 15, 20,
25, 30 and even 40 years. Amazing? Now that's family.
— Ducky O'Toole

the employees became fearful for their jobs and worried about their families and livelihoods. Knowing of their concerns, the Habers called an all-staff meeting to comfort them.

Even when something displeased Edgar about an employee, he was always a gentleman and dispensed advice in an indirect way, even when a new employee arrived for work with a head full of unkempt hair tucked under his golf cap.

Ed Haber not only had a knack for teaching by storytelling, he seemed to enjoy sharing his experiences and successes with young people, many of whom learned lessons they applied long after leaving their employment at Quail.

Edgar's passion for golf drove him to invite anyone and everyone, from friends to complete strangers, to come to Quail Lodge and play golf or learn how to play golf. His enthusiasm was contagious.

As the business paid off its debts and became successful, Terry and Edgar purchased a condominium in Hawaii in order to provide a place where they could award employees for their excellence. They provided an all-expense paid trip to Maui for a week of rest and relaxation, which served to thank employees and also increased the employees' loyalty and appreciation.

Edgar never berated his staff and rarely expressed displeasure with a guest, but if a customer poorly treated a maid or greens keeper, he could rise up as if a knight in shining armor on a white stallion to protect them from harm or abuse.

ROUND-A-BOUT LESSONS

Mr. Haber had a way of explaining things to you, too. Like, if I was doing something wrong he didn't reprimand me. He would call me in to his office or we'd talk some place outside the shop, at a table or somewhere private, and he'd tell a story about 'someone.' but you really knew that someone was you, though you couldn't prove it because it was always in a round about way. Nor did you take offense because the talk always ended well. But whatever story or lesson, it was always really about you. He never scolded me or anyone, not ever. He was always very kind — and, very smart.

— Mary Bayless

BUSTED

When I was hired at Quail, I was just a kid and I had long hair, so I tucked it under my baseball cap. On my first day on the job, I was cleaning the pool when this man comes up and introduces himself as the Chief Quail, and just started talking to me. I wondered who the hell this guy was until he said, 'Oh, I see that you're going to be needing a haircut soon.'

— Mike Ochs

A MENTOR OF MENTORS

I applied for a job at Quail when I was only 19 and worked there for 17 years. My first day of work I was told to meet Mr. Haber, or Chief Quail, or Eagle One, as he was called. I hadn't even started work but figured I must have done something wrong because, with 250 employees at Quail, I wondered why the owner would take the time to meet with me? I was pretty nervous, to say the least, and to my relief, we talked a little about golf and our meeting was short and pleasant. Later I learned that he made a point to meet every new employee on his or her first day of work. Throughout the years all of the employees felt good whenever Mr. Haber came into a room, flashing his easy smile; he was a magnet that drew people to him, put everyone to ease and made us enjoy our work. When I signed on I had no idea he would be my inspiration for golf to become my lifelong career. After recently moving to my new position with the Pebble Beach Company, I became even more aware that everything I ever learned about the golf business was due to Mr. Haber's patience; he was a remarkable teacher. He was a mentor of mentors.

— Casey Christensen

FROM THE BOTTOM UP

Well, I'd say, first, get a job and go to work somewhere, then figure out what needs to be done. If it's the golf business, sign on as a cart boy and clean carts, clean clubs, pick up golf balls on the range — do everything at the very lowest level, then get into the pro shop and move up. If it's a hotel, go to work in the kitchen as a dishwasher, or the front desk or bell desk so you learn what it takes to make a hotel work. You need to start at the bottom because you can't learn from the top down. You need to know the small details and little problems so when you're the manager or boss, you can solve the big problems and won't make the little mistakes that cause the money to go out the back door.

— Edgar Haber

There are literally countless stories from employees who received kindnesses of every sort from the Habers, from surprise visits to the hospital, to allowing an office worker bring her child to work and, for more than one employee, to volunteer financial assistance.

FREE LESSONS

When I worked in the pro shop Mr. Haber taught me how to play golf because he said golfing taught you about manners and honesty. Now, many years later, I have designed my own golf course and share the many lessons I learned from him with my own employees, and we are all the better for it.

— Clara Hardesty

TEACHING WITH THE CARROT, NOT THE STICK

Not once in 30 years did I ever hear Edgar raise his voice to an employee. And never once did I hear him lecture an employee. His style of management and employee relationships was to have a conversation, an equal conversation where it was back and forth. Usually, at some point, he would asked the employee some questions that required him or her to figure out the answers themselves, without preaching or lecturing or berating. I don't recall him ever laying off an employee due to tough times or lack of business. He never missed a payroll and always found a way to pay a dividend each year to his stockholders. He and Terry had a special way of creating a feeling of family and caring for their entire staff by the wonderful company parties, by the quiet gifts that would show up whenever an employee had a baby and by the sponsored trips to Hawaii, not to mention the many gifts to employees that were never, ever mentioned, as was his nature. One example of making lemonade was the kid who got caught ripping donuts in the golf course with his car. Rather than calling the Sheriff and prosecuting him, Edgar asked the kid to come out and repair the damage; then, seeing what a great job the kid had done, he offered him a job with the greens crew. The young man became one of the top employees for 12 years and then went on to start his own successful landscape business.

— Lawson Little

THE BABY IN THE OFFICE

I was working at Quail as the director of marketing and public relations when my baby daughter was diagnosed with an extremely rare disease and could not be left alone. At the time my husband was the assistant manager, but the doctor bills were enormous, so we both needed to work but I also needed to give her constant care, so we concluded that I had to quit work to care for her. When I told Mr. Haber I had to quit and why, I was astonished when he said, 'Look, why not bring her to work with you?' So I did and I placed her basket right on my desk. Whenever I had to leave my desk, the other women in the office were delighted to watch over her. Now that's pretty amazing!

— Jeanie Gould

THE DOWN PAYMENT

I began as a bus boy at Quail in 1975. Gee, that's almost 40 years ago! I was a Vietnam vet with a family and new baby due, so money was always in short supply. I had only worked at Quail for one week, but somehow Mr. Haber found out I needed a down payment for a house. He called me into his office and gave me a check for $1,000. He said it wouldn't be taken from my check and that I could pay it off when I was able to and with no interest.

— Rudy Quidileg

ENOUGH, MA'AM

Mr. Haber rarely got directly involved with guest issues, and was always even tempered, but he was very protective of his staff. One day as he was walking through the front desk, a rather affluent guest was loudly berating the reservations girl for some minor error. Edgar stopped short and said, 'Enough! There's no reason to beat her up.' The woman asked, 'Well, and who the hell are you?' Edgar replied politely but firmly, 'I am the owner,' and continued, 'whatever she did, she didn't do it on purpose. She made a mistake. Mistakes happen. And we will do everything possible to make it right.' As I recall he sent the rather disagreeable guest some champagne and desert with his card and a nice note.

— Steve Gould

ALWAYS THERE

Once I got into a bad car accident and Mr. Haber showed up at the hospital to see me, which was kinda embarrassing, but nice to know he was there for me, especially because at that time Quail had over 250 employees. He was always there for us.

— Rudy Quidileg

LOYALTY

During interviews for this book, when asked how the Habers retained so many faithful employees for year after year, almost all current and former employees referred to working at Quail as if it were a family. Many reasons were given for the employee loyalty and longevity, including: being proud to work for nice people in a quality environment, being treated with respect and kindness, having fun in a playful if hard-working environment and many said it was "the little things," and each one had a different story, some of which follow.

CHIVAS ON THE ROCKS, PLEASE

Mr. Haber put me in charge of the helicopter rides and of taking care of Arnold Palmer, Gary Player and other golfers who stayed at Quail during the US Open. He told Mr. Palmer it was my 21st birthday and they invited me for my very first drink at the bar. Mr. Haber explained, 'Now this is called a screwdriver, it's got some clear stuff called Vodka in some orange juice.' Then I said, 'I'd rather have a Chivas on the rocks,' and both men began cracking up.

— Sidney Reade

FISHING WITH MY FOLKS

When my folks came to visit, Mr. Haber invited us to go up to his lake and go fishing. So we all three borrowed his rods and fished for two hours without even a nibble. A few days later I'm driving by his house and see him sitting on the dock fishing, so I went over to thank him for being so nice to my folks, and I watched him cast seven times, catch seven fish, and throw all seven back into the lake.

— Mike Ochs

BREWS FOR THE CREWS

When I started here, every Friday Mr. Haber brought a case of beer to the grounds keeping crew. But laws changed in the 90s and as manager then I had to advise him about the liability of his generosity. He fought me for two years and still came with a case every Friday, but I think his attorney advised him otherwise and, reluctantly, he finally stopped bringing beer, but he still kept on with his Friday visits to the crew shack.

— Denis Kerr

KEEPING THE FAMILY TOGETHER

I used to do a couple of things like the phony pairing trick just to keep him on his toes…you know, just let him know he wasn't such a hot shot. And we always had a good time. We had a good relationship. A lot of times…I appreciated him much more, of course, when I didn't work for him, but I did appreciate him when I was here because it was a steady job that was a lot of fun and he gave me lots of leeway. Every night after work about 20 employees would go up to the bar and have drinks with everybody else. It was a family. And he kept people around because he'd be up there with us, and we'd play liars dice or whatever, and he was just…well, he had a way about him. I never met anybody before who could keep people together like that. He solved interpersonal spats because everybody had a fiefdom and wanted to run their own thing. Often my golf plans would step on the superintendent's toes, and the superintendent's would step on the Lodge gardener's toes and, you know, Edgar would solve all these little differences. As one big family we understood that. He was a master. He was a master of organizing people and understanding people, and what they would and wouldn't do. Essentially, he was the papa of the family and Terry was the mama.

— Bob Holmes

The Secrets Of Success

*You can learn more
about a man in nine holes
of golf than in a
boardroom for a year.*

— Edgar Haber

Edgar noted matter-of-factly in his interview that he was only a mediocre student whose marks were not high enough for him to enter college. He didn't say so, but it was not for lack of intelligence that his grades were substandard, and one would surmise given his future successes that high school simply did not engage his interests; perhaps he was more focused on mastering the game of golf than he was on mastering his text books. He did spend a year and a half in a business school in the evenings, but during the day he continued to practice and play golf and study his scorecards.

During his last year in the military, during his off-duty time, Edgar created his first of two business ventures, the monocular, or Sporting Scope, and the *Park Merced News* with classifieds and news tidbits. It was there he first succeeded in business, first by selling something nobody had ever seen before and second by seeing and fulfilling a need.

After moving to Carmel Valley in 1957, his later business ventures followed the same pattern. The *Carmel Valley Sun* newspaper was a variation of the *Lake Merced* mimeograph; the unsuccessful Carmel Valley Theatre and the successful Valley Liquors Store, were attempts to fulfill things lacking in the community. But when the opportunity arose to buy a dairy farm and create a golf course, home sites and a hotel, Edgar employed what he had learned and engaged some other sixth sense to accomplish something on a magnitude that he had never done before.

As gleaned from over 80 interviews from people of all walks of life, both Edgar and wife Terry had many qualities that contributed to their business successes. The stories, one-by-one, begin to form a picture of his business acumen. It appears the main quality for their success was their dedication to quality itself in every aspect of conducting a business, which is perhaps best understood by reading the actual anecdotes without editorial comment. The general categories for the Habers' business success are customer service, frugality, common sense, opportunism, honor and diplomacy, a few anecdotes of which are quoted.

CUSTOMER SERVICE

One of the key categories of the Mobil Five-Star Award was customer service, but the Habers did not need a checklist to provide extraordinary service for their customers, which included everything from satisfying quirky restaurant requests, to speaking directly with guests and to solving service problems with simple but brilliant actions. Of the countless stories told, the following are three of the more precious.

EGGS BENNY
General Jimmy Doolittle's favorite breakfast was eggs benedict at Quail Lodge. But as Jimmy got older, an early breakfast was inconvenient for him, and he didn't show up for his 'eggs benny,' as he fondly called them, until early afternoon, which became so late the Covey staff began to refuse to serve breakfast orders because it was lunch time. I mentioned this casually to Edgar one day and he promptly advised the staff that no matter what time of day General Doolittle arrived, they were instructed to serve him his eggs benny. And so it was forever after.
— Arthur Ragen, Colonel, USAF, ret.

YES, I'M MR. HABER
As we passed by the front desk on the way to a lunch meeting, the woman at the desk called out, 'Mr. Haber, I have a guest on the phone who has a problem, what should I do?' He took the phone and all he had to say was, 'Hello, yes, this is Mr. Haber and, yes, I and the owner of the property,' and right then the problem went away.
— Tom Gray

FRUGALITY

Sometimes it takes more judgment than simply to declare that something or other suits the tired British cliché, "penny wise and pound foolish," or don't focus on minutiae and lose sight of the big picture. Edgar had a distinctly unique way of looking at employee overtime in the hotel business. He also figured out that it would be better to spend less rather than more money on a specific sprinkler head because it had another, unseen quality that gave it more value. And, to press his point to a manager using miles of adding machine tape to tally the inventory, he mused humorously about the need for someone to invent a way to use the other side of the tape.

COMMON SENSE

Ever the optimist, Edgar was also ever the pragmatist and understood human nature, such as getting someone involved in a problem for which he knew the solution but allowed them to take credit when they came around to the same solution. He had a keen sense of business and could look at a business plan and know at once whether it was viable or not. He could also take a complex business plan and reduce it to the simplest of terms that anyone could understand. When it came to mistakes made by others, he seemed to have more than a common sense of optimism by perceiving the upside of any error.

When correcting an employee about a mistake or their job in general, Edgar patiently explained the percentages and how profit was determined for their particular department. And whenever possible, albeit indirectly and never touting his own accomplishments, he shared his philosophy of success, which was to set and accomplish goals, then to work and earn his way.

WHAT IT TAKES

I had been a club professional at MPCC and then a new role as ambassador at Pebble Beach, but when the company sold I applied at Quail, thinking that because my great experience, Edgar Haber would offer me a salary as large as the lotto. In the interview he did not offer me a lot of money and explained that nobody had ever given him anything. He gave me a primer on how he made it: everything he got, he earned; everything he earned, he worked for; everything he worked for he accomplished; and everything he accomplished was because he had set a goal, and he always reached his goal. And that was the message: the simple steps of a simple process.

— Ducky O'Toole

BY THE NUMBERS

Edgar Haber had tremendous instinct and a tremendous command of numbers. He could read a profit and loss upside down and a balance sheet from the bottom up. So when he was having the conversation with an employee, it would end up with a question about why this percentage is a little higher than last month on the cost of sales or something like that. He made sure the manager knew the appropriate percentage to look at and when it changes one direction or another, which is why the employee needed to know why to make the correct decisions. So if your cost of sales is too high, maybe from the bar, you know, that'll trigger one of three things and the manager needs to know which one. That was the type of insight and training he taught his staff.

— Lawson Little

LOSE ONE, WIN ONE

In early 1981 I was trying to play golf professionally on the tour. I took lessons from Ben Doyle at Quail and got to know the folks in the pro shop, especially when Bob Holmes was in the shop. He let me hit balls in trade for gathering range balls and cleaning carts. It felt so good to be there that I abandoned my goal of going pro. When Holmes left, it was hard to replace him, so I asked Mr. Haber for the job, but he was cautious and offered me to intern for a year before I got it. One day I had a major boondoggle with the Western Italian Group that had an annual tournament. It started as 80 players then grew to 120, then 140 and finally 150 players and we didn't have that many carts so we rented more and still ran out. We had an arrangement with members to credit their account if we ever rented their cart because they rented by the year, which worked well until the day of that tournament. We needed one more cart but couldn't reach the member, so I went ahead anyway and made the judgment call, wouldn't you know, on a day he'd never played before, the member showed up and was piping hot mad. He sounded off to Edgar, who called me in. I was expecting to get holy hell but instead he said, 'Laird, it was a bad deal what you did here today, but although you lost one for the membership, you won one for the company. Well done.' He was always able to see both sides of an issue or problem and react with balance.

— Laird Small

71

OPPORTUNISM

An opportunist exploits circumstances to gain an immediate advantage. Ed Haber was an opportunist in the most creative sense of the word and his timing was impeccable. When he arrived in Carmel Valley, he discovered a rural area sparsely populated with farms and ranches producing crops and cattle that was at the very edge of change of livelihoods and lifestyles. He was able to perceive and fulfill the changing needs of the departing and incoming generation.

In addition to establishing its first newspaper, movie theatre and liquor store, he was able to envision a golf course and hotel in the site of a failing dairy farm, the natural beauty of which he preserved by dedicating the golf course into permanent scenic easement which, in turn, allowed him to consolidate the home sites. After seizing upon these opportunities, on behalf of the community, he saw the need to create a fire department, support law enforcement and establish paramedics in the valley.

Sometimes it is the smaller and more humorous seizing of opportunities that provide insight into the larger man, such as: parking his vehicle prominently in front of the Pebble Beach Lodge during major tournaments to advertise Quail Lodge; or denying the request for a customer's room refund in order to create a long-term relationship; or having the hotel bell man wash the lodge guests' car windows during the night; or casually overhearing construction workers needing rocks for a project and offering to provide them from the nearby river; or by offering his pond to store and save fish during a drought, then enjoying fishing for those left behind. With Edgar, timely opportunism was an art form.

PARKING AT PEBBLE

When Mr. Haber went to Pebble Beach for a large tournament, he always drove his two-tone gold and black Mercedes station wagon with the red light on top with the prominent Quail Lodge signs on the doors. Somehow he always managed to have the valet park it in the most prominent place at the entrance to The Lodge, perhaps because he told the attendants to have it 'at the ready' in the event of an emergency. He would drive players to and from Pebble, but would always return the car to be parked in same place. From time to time, for mysterious reasons, the battery, the fuel pump or other mechanical thing would fail and the vehicle would have to stay parked there overnight. He could not have gotten better advertising for Quail Lodge with the thousands of tournament visitors and it didn't cost him a dime.

— Mary Bayless

ROCK? I GOT ROCK

When my dad had his Equitable Building in Monterey, we often lunched at the Casa Munras where a lot of businessmen dined. If you knew my dad, you'd know when he sat down at a table with you, one ear was listening to you and the other ear was often bent toward the next table. That day he overhead that Granite had gotten the bid for the interchange at Highway One at Pebble Beach, but they had to haul rock clear from the Salinas River. So, not to miss an opportunity, as was his way, he leaned over and said, 'I have a lot of river rock down at the dairy farm in Carmel Valley, so why don't you get it from me? It will save you a bunch in hauling costs and clean out the river for me.' So Granite set up a scraper operation and crusher plant where the clubhouse is today. They mined all the rock they needed for their project and in doing so they lowered the riverbed considerably for my dad.

— John Haber Splittorf

WE NEVER REFUND

Once I refunded money to a lodge guest and Mr. Haber was upset. But instead of firing me, he calmly explained his philosophy. 'A complaint could be either bogus or a genuine grievance. Instead of refunding them, he said, we should invite them back for the wonderful experience that they should have had in the first place. For those who don't come back, well, they just wanted their money back in the first place, so we don't want them back. But for those who do return, we make certain they have a wonderful experience, so they will come back again and again.' Over my years as assistant manager, we never had many unhappy people, but the few who were, we complimented their next visit, for whatever reason, and those guests became loyal converts and our greatest fans who sang our praises and brought in new business. It was a philosophy that served us well for many years in our Five-Star property.

— Steve Gould

HONOR

It is said these days that honor is a thing of the past. Well, that might be, but it was an integral part of the makeup of Edgar Haber's character. Essentially, in his old-fashioned sense of honor, a man's handshake was his word, even if the result became disadvantageous, such as honoring a construction bid despite a lower bid that came in later. Contention between people is often an unpleasant experience in life, but as time passes, it is more honorable to forgive than prolong, as was the case with the successors of Edgar's rival neighbor.

When a contractor makes an honest error, it is more honorable to work out a solution and let it go than punish him. Why? Because in business, there is always a tomorrow. Likewise, when you have someone in a "pinch point," negotiating fairly with them is the honorable thing to do. There are many examples of Edgar's old-fashioned belief in honor and fair play; following are but a few examples as shared by others.

NOT THE CHEAPEST BID, BUT THE BEST

One construction company had always done Quail's large construction projects but when the request went out for the $5 million Quail Meadow infrastructure project, I submitted a bid. When I went to Mr. Haber's office, we had never met, and told him I didn't mind investing my time bidding for such a large job, but I needed his word that if we were the low bidder, we would get the work. He assured me we would. When our bid came in as the lowest, unknown to me at the time, my competitor was on the phone immediately to Ed and lowered their price. When we met to sign the contract, Ed said, 'You know, you were the low bidder at the time you bid the job, but you are not the low bidder today because your competitor lowered their price, but I told them, if they could lower their price after the bidding, why didn't they lower it before?' Despite the fact he could have gotten the work done cheaper, Edgar honored his promise and kept his word. He was a man of honor.

— Don Chapin

TWO BULLS IN A PASTURE

Arthur Oppenheimer was a rather mercurial character who may have had a wish in life to see how many people he could aggravate. He would let his cattle out to trample the greens on Edgar's new golf course and even sued Edgar twice over use of the San Carlos Bridge, although he lost both times. Even when Edgar and Terry built their home in what is now Quail Meadows, he refused them an easement for a telephone line, so they had to use walkie-talkies. Some unpleasant history had developed before my partner and I bought Rancho San Carlos from Arthur to develop what became the Santa Lucia Preserve. In a sense we wound up stepping into Arthur's shoes, which were sometimes a little tight and often rather painful, so we had to overcome some bad history when we met Edgar for the first time, but he never held any of that bad history against us. He was always the gentleman and we became very good friends.

— Tom Gray

SO THAT'S HOW YOU DO IT

Mallard Lake at the Lodge began leaking water soon after it was completed. I was in the meeting with the contractor to resolve the issue. It was their mistake and their problem to solve, but Mr. Haber worked out a painless deal for them. I asked why he let them off the hook and he explained, 'Well, that's the way you do business. It's a team effort and somewhere down the line we'll do business again.'

— Denis Kerr

DIPLOMACY

The art of diplomacy is a rare but often necessary quality to accomplish difficult tasks, especially when dealing with politicians and regulators. Edgar was a master of this art form as attested by several anecdotes and observations. When confronted with the immovable object of a planning commissioner who withheld approval of the Quail Meadows project, all Edgar needed for her approval was to satisfy her concern, albeit unrealistic, that the new subdivision would bring people's pets who, in turn, would harass the area wildlife. His solution was simply to suggest and implement a "dog run" where the domestic animals would not "harass the wild animals."

THE DOG RUN

*When Ed and Terry were developing Quail Meadows,
there was one planning commissioner who seemed to say no
to everything — never yes to anything. She loved wild animals
and during a tour of the property, she remarked, 'You know,
the worst thing people do when putting subdivisions in
undeveloped areas, they let their dogs and cats run wild and kill
all the wildlife; that's horrible, just horrible.' And so Edgar said,
'What would you do?' And she says, 'Well, I'd set aside a place, a
run, a pet run, a big area where you could take your pets and let
them run free.' And so into the general plan we incorporated a
special fenced-in area with a sign, 'The (name withheld) Animal
Exercise Area.' To this day, the dog run has never been used,
although it has been meticulously maintained.*

— Anthony Lombardo, Esq.

Providing adequate water for the Quail Meadows subdivision was another diplomatic coup involving diplomacy using wit and opportunity. To create water credits for the subdivision, Edgar replaced the aging golf course irrigation system and applied the water savings to Quail Meadows, another win-win that diplomatically solved two problems simultaneously.

WIN-WIN, THE WATER

*The Golf Club at Quail Lodge as it is now known has always been
renowned for the condition of the course. It wasn't always that
way. In the late 70s, the water system had run its course and
needed to be replaced. The cost of installing an irrigation system
for 130 acres is very costly and Edgar always looked for the best
deal in anything he did. At the same time, Quail Meadows was in
the planning stage and the subject of water supply for the
development was paramount for approval by the Board of
Supervisors. Where will the water come from for the development?
The property comprising the subdivision was called Porter's Bowl,
which had a low point where the Habers built their house, and
that was where the cattle had come to drink; it was a pond in the
winter but only a mud hole in the summer, but obviously not
adequate to satisfy the Supervisors approval much less provide
enough water for the subdivision. Hmm…? What if Quail were to
completely replace the golf course watering system with a new,
efficient system that would save more water than was needed and
the excess could be transferred to Quail Meadows to offset the
shortfall? We were probably going to replace the old sprinkler
system anyway, but Edgar used that as leverage for the
development. Save the water. Another win-win!*

— Bob Holmes

Perhaps the most diplomatic of Edgar's persuasive qualities was involving people with the problem so they could take ownership by solving it, for which they always received the credit and Edgar achieved his goal.

GETTING FROM NO TO YES

If you ask someone for their advice on something, it's hard for them to be against you when you come back and do what they say. So, he was expert at getting elected officials and bureaucrats to support whatever he was doing on the basis that he would say, 'Geez, I don't know. What do you think I ought to do here? What would you do if it were you?'

— Anthony Lombardo, Esq.

Diplomacy is designed to generate consensus and preempt problems. It was a key element in Edgar's *modus operandi* that came natural to him, which he executed flawlessly most of the time, and made him a master in the art of the deal.

WHEN A CAMEL IS NOT A RACEHORSE

Nobody succeeds alone. I learned a lot from Ed's wisdom and support for The Preserve. When you want to get something done, you need consent, not consensus. Consensus gets you a camel when you want a racehorse.

— Tom Gray

ART OF THE DEAL

I probably learned more about how to be a good lawyer from Edgar than by going to law school. He mentored me on the art of the deal, about which he was an expert. His tutelage on how to get along with people and how to get people to do what you want them to do was a big part of it.

— Anthony Lombardo, Esq.

CHALLENGES

Not all of Edgar's business affairs were rosy and without challenge, and not every business associate was friendly and with the same interests, such as "The Farmer." When Edgar purchased the property from Dwight Morrow, in order to configure the golf course the way he wanted, he needed a few more acres to complete numbers 11 and 12 golf holes on the land to the immediate south and east of the dairy farm.

Louis Wolters, whose father had homesteaded the land many years before, owned the property. They were no-nonsense farmers who sewed and tilled the rich, river bottomland and earned their living by selling their crops. For years they operated a successful fruit and vegetable stand in a shack along the roadside in mid-Carmel Valley. Perhaps it was their dislike of such a frivolous thing as a golf course being built beside their historic farmland that unsettled them and caused their cantankerous behavior and Edgar's prolonged frustration and aggravation.

Edgar's initial resources had been committed to the purchase and development of the dairy farm property, but he nevertheless approached Wolters about buying the portion he needed to complete the desired golf course layout, but the farmer said his family homestead land was not for sale, though he could lease it for a tidy sum, should he desire. Edgar had little choice but to enter into a 50-year lease agreement that needed renegotiation every five years, which over the next 45 years became a major thorn in Edgar's otherwise patient side from which he suffered considerably.

During the 1930s Arthur Oppenheimer was a successful businessman from San Francisco. As the story goes, at his yacht club, Arthur met George King, a common man who could fix anything but who always wanted to be a rancher, so he was hired to run what Oppenheimer had renamed the Rancho San Carlos. For reasons unknown, 20 years later, Oppenheimer's foreman and Edgar did not get along well, perhaps because the cattle ranch foreman and gentleman golfer simply had personality differences. Or, perhaps it was because the foreman was a born-again cowboy who thought his cows belonged in the valley more than a golf course. Regardless of why, tensions between the two neighbors often ran high.

THE FARMER

As we worked to nail down all legalities for the golf course, we had to lease the east end of the property, portions of holes 11 and 12, from Louis Wolters, whose organic farm land had been growing lettuce for decades. Tom Hudson was the attorney for 'The Farmer,' as he came to be somewhat unaffectionately known, and we either had to sign a tough lease or redesign the course by using the 40 acres across San Carlos Road, which was not a good golf course option for Edgar. Every five years for the next 45 years we had to undergo expensive appraisals and lengthy negotiations, each term costing more than the previous. The lease was always a thorn in Edgar's side, but with everything else in his life going so well, his tolerance was stoic.

— Myron 'Doc' Etienne

Arthur died in the late 1940s and his son, Arthur Jr., took over the ranch. Although he let the foreman King continue to run the ranch, the young heir only oversaw the operation without much direct involvement. Yet, despite the change of ownership, the enmity continued between Edgar and the foreman. One wonders whether their conflict was caused by the difference between a cowboy and a golfer, or perhaps because of the different lifestyles associated with cattle grazing and golfers playing.

The challenges continued with the irascible neighbor, but this time the conflict went from physical to legal. Myron "Doc" Etienne became the Habers' legal counsel after meeting him at the Pacific Biological Laboratory, which later came to be known as Doc Rickett's Lab. Doc recalls being with him at the dairy farm early on, "when the whole dream thing got underway."

Years before, to cross the Carmel River from the Valley Road to his Rancho San Carlos, Oppenheimer bought an abandoned bridge in the Sierras and his foreman transported and installed it on San Carlos Road, which is owned and maintained by the county but Oppenheimer was nonetheless proprietary about its use and seemed to enjoy flexing his muscles.

Years later, when the Habers decided to build a home and new subdivision in Quail Meadows, the neighbor once again filed a cause of action that objected to additional traffic use.

In Monterey County, California, and perhaps elsewhere, there are many challenges for anyone who wants to develop anything, anywhere, anytime. Edgar Haber was a master of cultivating relationships and providing creative solutions to what some might call wildly unreasonable regulatory requirements, but he was never discouraged and his ingenuity was surpassed only by his patience, if often taxed to its limit.

Often the only way to overcome challenges, regardless of their source, is to exercise faith in one's self and fellow man, take a deep breath and simply move forward with the optimistic faith that, with good intentions and good works, everything will work out.

STANDOFF AT THE 4TH GREEN

When my father was building the golf course, the fairways and greens had just been seeded and fresh sprouts of green grasses were shooting up everywhere. We lived in a condo on the 4th fairway at the time and I recall the Oppenheimer cattle used to break out of Rancho San Carlos and ravage the fresh new grasses. They got out on what became an unusually regular basis. It was kinda like the cowboy versus the businessman. He and my dad didn't much like each other. But it soon became suspicious because the ranch was about 20,000 acres and the cattle had more land to feed on than they'd ever eat, so why did they get out on the golf course? It happened so often that it became obvious to my dad, who had been very patient up to then, that the foreman was intentionally letting the cattle out so they could graze on the new grasses and hassle him, being the new guy next door, he guessed. Besides, the golf course wasn't necessarily great chomping ground because the grass was only an inch high. So one day we saw the cattle strolling down from the ranch toward the fourth green. I just happened to be at his house that day and saw my dad pull out his M-1 carbine that was his during the army and load it with a clip of shells. We walked up the fairway to the green and there were five head of cattle. There were three cowboys riding horseback with rifles in the scabbards of their saddles. It seemed like something right out of the movies to me. And my father said, 'If those cattle get onto that green, I'm going to shoot them.' And they said, 'If you shoot the cattle, we're going to shoot you.' I didn't know what was going to happen. I didn't know who was going shoot whom. I didn't know if my father was going to shoot the cattle or they would shoot my father and which way it would go. So it was a stand off at the fourth green. Other than the three cowboys, only my father and I were there, alone. Anyway, the cows came right up to the edge of the green and, I don't know exactly how it all worked out, but they did not step one foot on that green. The cowboys herded off the cattle and we never saw them or their cattle on the golf course again.

— Warren Haber

TWO TOMCATS IN A GUNNY SACK

Ed's southern neighbor, Arthur Oppenheimer, owned the San Carlos Ranch. They were like two tomcats in a gunnysack. They did not get along at all. Edgar had been instrumental in the development of Hacienda Carmel, a 300-unit retirement community immediately west of Quail Lodge. After the first 175 units were built, construction began on the last 125, but Oppenheimer put a 25-ton limit on the bridge he owned that crossed the river on San Carlos Road, which was the only way to access Hacienda at that time. I was asked as their legal counsel what to do and I told them to run the trucks, and the next morning Oppenheimer filed the suit and sent a couple of hotshot, Harvard-and-Yale, attorneys from San Francisco to deal with we country bumpkins. Well, we proved that Mr. Oppenheimer had run many loads of cattle and rock over the bridge that far exceeded 25 tons, which destroyed his argument, and the hotshot attorneys fled back to the city.

— Myron 'Doc' Etienne

IF WE DON'T DO IT, WHO WILL?

In the late 1980s we finally got tentative approval for the Quail Meadows homes development. By 1990 we had worked through all 104 planning conditions and were ready to break ground. However, the entire country moved into the mess of a major recession and we needed to make the decision whether to shut down or move forward to take out a loan for the $8 million project. We met with the board of directors and they were very reluctant to move forward because of the economy. After they had finished Edgar said, 'Well, what we need to do is to create opportunities for people and put them to work; this project will generate enough money to feed at least 50 families for three or four years. We need to move forward in order to go beyond. If we don't do it, who will?' The board approved unanimously to proceed with the project. Quail Meadows has been acclaimed as one of the finest small communities in the United States. Edgar and Terry were always so proud that they were able to do this with neither having graduated from college.

— Lawson Little

A DEVELOPER HAS NO FRIENDS

When you're in the development business, such as building Quail Lodge, you really don't know who your friends are, except for your very good ones. Beyond that, you really don't know. It's a crapshoot. Why somebody is cultivating a relationship with you, you don't know why because some people want something from you and others want to take something away from you. It was not easy when Edgar built Quail Lodge, but by the time he built Quail Meadows, he had earned his spurs and in many ways paved the way for us to build The Preserve.

— Tom Gray

More than once Edgar faced unforeseeable challenges that required creative solutions, such as the complex subject of water and water availability throughout California, but especially on the Monterey Peninsula, where the issue is as problematic as its solution is obtuse.

For years the Habers lived in condos and homes located on the golf course where they were engaged in daily contact with the employees, residents, members, golfers and lodge guest. Although they enjoyed people and the camaraderie of constant interactions, there came a time when they yearned for a home separate yet near the resort.

Their friend and attorney, Doc Etienne, also represented the owner of the adjacent Corona Ranch, which adjoined the Porter Bowl property. One day Edgar and Terry walked up on a small lot near the property entrance, which they had sold to Rancho San Carlos, then later bought it back. It was atop that beautiful knoll they decided to build their home in the area and pursue consolidating the two properties to create Quail Meadows.

It appeared that every time Edgar was challenged with a problem, he engaged his thinking and came up a creative, if unusual solution, which more often than not solved two problems simultaneously.

WATER PROBLEM? WHAT WATER PROBLEM?

One day as Edgar and I were driving through Quail Meadows, he stopped the car at Quail Lake and told me the water story. The original depressed area between what became the barn and his house was a sump, called Porter Lake, where the cows drank that was full of water in the winter and muddy in the summer, so he knew there was water below. After buying the property and planning the development, one of his first improvements was to build a lake, as he had done with the 10 lakes on the golf course, by digging a shallow well and installing a pump, then sealing the bottom and building a small waterfall. During the permit process when touring the planners through the property, as they neared the lake area one asked, 'Well, what about the water, Mr. Haber?' About that time they were approaching the lake, now complete with a small aeration fountain pumping water into the air, and he said, 'Water? What problem?'

— Gary Koeppel

Edgar and station wagon with red light beside Porter Lake

ANOTHER CHALLENGE, ANOTHER DREAM

Edgar and I were always moving around between living in the condos and houses at Quail and a house in the valley, so we thought it would be nice to have a house together and nearby, but outside of the subdivision. I didn't want to live on the golf course because I figured I'd never see him and we'd never have any privacy. So we started looking for a place and our head gardener took us up to a beautiful piece of land in what is now Quail Meadows. The property was known as the Porter Bowl, about 640 acres or so, and right in the middle of it was a mud slough in the summer and natural pond in the winter where the cows migrated and drank. We eventually got together with Stuyvesant Fish II and bought the piece, which became Quail Meadows.

—Terry Haber

WIN-WIN

When the Habers first created the Quail Meadows subdivision, it was still somewhat remote and they weren't getting much police protection. They had a gate and built a guardhouse but were unable to afford a gate guard. Edgar surmised that the Sheriff Department could use an out-station in that part of the valley, so he offered them use of the gatehouse where they could monitor calls, have coffee and write their reports, all the while with their patrol car sitting in full view, providing full security at no cost. Now, who would have thought of that? He got protection and the sheriff got a sub-station. Brilliant.

— Judge John Phillips

The Haber's Quail Meadows house above Quail Meadows Lake, formerly Porter Lake.

Chief Quail

When an opponent gained the advantage, Edgar would remark, "Now I've got him just where he wants me!"

— Edgar Haber

A person's character establishes behavior and determines actions. One could wax and wane about the qualities of Edgar Haber's character as a leader, but perhaps the more revealing and credible insights about Chief Quail are expressed by the many people who knew him as a result of their personal or professional relationship, as revealed in the following anecdotes. It appears that Edgar's most notable characteristics were his love for animals and in being a good citizen and gentleman; he practiced his belief in fair play and kindness and he modestly shared the lessons he had learned with those who sought his mentoring.

Edgar with three relatives.

FOR THE LOVE OF ANIMALS

Anyone knowing Edgar was aware of his love for animals. His Golden Retriever dogs were constant friends wherever he went, in his office, golf cart, restaurant and from time to time even the swimming pool. There are many stories about him and animals, ranging from modestly humorous to outright hilarious.

CHOOSING A RELATIVE
Acquiring a dog may be the only opportunity a human ever has to choose a relative.
— Edgar Haber

BONDING WITH DORIS
Knowing how Edgar felt about animals created a great bond between us. I shall be forever grateful that he was a director on the board of our Doris Day Animal League.
— Doris Day

HOLLYWOOD AT QUAIL
It was a Doris Day benefit, but it also benefited Quail. Edgar and Doris worked together with Lonnie Anderson, Suzanne Summers and Clint Eastwood. It was the first time we did something like that and was, as always, a huge success.
— Jeanie Gould

A DOG'S BIRTHDAY

Edgar loved his dogs and told me once,
'a dog will never turn on you, even if you forget his birthday.'
— Steve Gould

MAX AND THE SKUNK

When my father died he left behind a young Golden Retriever
named Max and Uncle Ed, as I and others fondly called him,
agreed to take him in. Max was a young and rambunctious
pup, full of energy and was as mischievous as could be.
The next day Terry phoned me and said he had gone outside in
the middle of the night, brought a dead skunk inside and
jumped into Edgar's bed, causing quite the havoc.
— Laird Small

POOL CLOSED, MA'AM

When his best friend, Kenzie his dog, had back surgery,
the veterinary surgeon recommended swimming as the best
exercise for a fast recovery, so Mr. Haber took him to the pool
below his office for a swim. One day a lady hotel guest
complained and the Health Department said he couldn't let
a dog swim in a public pool, so whenever Mr. Haber took
Kenzie for a swim he'd put up a sign that read: PRIVATE —
POOL CLOSED, then take it down after the swim.
Nancy Parsons

KENZIE'S GOLF CART

Kenzie was Mr. Haber's favorite dog who loved to ride in his golf
cart. In the afternoon whenever Edgar began to leave for a game,
he would spell out, 'Well, shall we play g-o-l-f?' As he spelled out
the word, the dog would dash from the room and be waiting
in the golf cart when Edgar arrived.
— Nancy Parsons

DOUBLING DOWN

I've been on the SPCA board forever and Edgar was one of our
animals' best friends. Ed personally matched the donations from
the first Haber Cup that doubled the gift to $14,000.
— Bob Evans

Acquiring a dog may be the only opportunity a human ever has to choose a relative.

GATHERING DUCK EGGS

I was amused to have ducks waddle up to the screen door of the large room of the new rambling country inn, Quail Lodge in Carmel Valley. The main lodge and golf course had 10 man-made lakes, all stocked with ducks, geese, quail and other fluttering wildlife. The owner/operator Edgar Haber explained, 'we couldn't very well be so close to the ocean and not have any water.' The lakes are so harmonious allied with the land that more and more birds keep coming all the time, winning the course recent recognition as a bona fide wild life refuge. During the duck-laying season, when land animals such as fox, opossum, raccoons, skunks, weasels and bobcats seek out the eggs as a delicacy, every day Haber and his golf course crew actually scooped out the eggs in nets, took them to the barn for incubation, and returned the chicks when they are old enough to fend for themselves. Now, that's something.

— Lee Tyler, Travel Writer, <u>San Jose Mercury News</u>

SLEEPING WITH THE DOGS

As Edgar got older, so did his dogs, one of which became blind and the other deaf. As a fellow neighbor in Quail Meadows, I'd often see him park on one of the downhill roads where the sun was shining on them, all three asleep, basking in the sun.

— Bob Evans

THE GOAT STORY

After Edgar and Terry built and moved into their home in Quail Meadows, Edgar learned that there were about 100 goats that had denuded all vegetation from one of the small islands off Santa Barbara. There was nothing left to eat so the military was going to remove the goats and kill them. Well, every animal lover in the country objected strenuously and Edgar thought they would reduce the brush for fire safely and had also heard that goats ate poison oak, which was abundant in Quail Meadows, so he exercised both his practical and charitable instincts and, before it became a subdivision, he offered to put the goats on his new ranch where they could graze freely and, hopefully, also eradicate the poison oak. The response was immediate. The humane people flew out a goat expert from Florida who herded them into a raft, floated them ashore where they were loaded on trucks and delivered to their new home. There was an enormous "Celebration of the Goats" with dozens of photographers whose pictures filled national newspapers. Edgar was a goat savior. The humane guy flew back to Florida and the goats ran excitedly into the thick brush of the ranch. But soon goats began to disappear as the mountain lions ate their fill of a new delicacy and by the end of the first year only half remained. Edgar was devastated, rounded up the remaining few and took them to the corral behind his home for safety. But when he awoke in the morning, a mountain lion had jumped the fencing and killed them all. For Edgar it was a sad day, indeed, as well as the end of the goat story.

— Myron 'Doc' Etienne, Jr., Esq.

CITIZENSHIP

Among the many people with whom I was fortunate to interviews for this book, many were prominent members of the community, all of whom had intriguing stories about citizen Haber, ranging from the most respected banker in the area, to an appointee of Ronald Reagan, a respected attorney and a famous WWII air force pilot, all of whom were friends and admirers whose comments are succinct and profound.

DESERVING OF A BOOK
*I've known and still know a lot of people on this Peninsula.
I can't think of one other person, with the possible exception of
Hank Ketchum, of everybody I've known that deserves to have
a book written about him.*
— Clay Larson

CITIZEN HABER
*Edgar rose from a modest start in life to become an icon of Carmel
Valley and the entire Monterey Peninsula. He has been chosen
and publicly recognized by his peers as one of this area's all-time
most outstanding citizens; he is truly a legend in his own time.*
— Gordon Paul Smith

DOOLITTLE OR DO A LOT
*Jimmy Doolittle, who conducted the 1942 air raid over Tokyo after
Pearl Harbor, once said to me, 'the only reason men were placed
on this planet was to improve things now and in the future' —
and that 'Ed Haber certainly fits into that mold.'*
— Brick Holstrom, a Tokyo Raider, USAF, General, Ret.

NO COMPS
*There is absolutely no one else in our community who can claim a
comparable record of achievement.*
— Myron 'Doc' Etienne, Jr., Esq.

GENTLEMAN

PAYING TO PLAY
*Edgar Haber was strongly influenced by his father who was
one of the many victims of the 1929 depression and had
always tried to convey the basic qualities of paying your way,
playing by the rules and acting like a gentleman.*
— Gary Koeppel

KENZIE'S ID CARD
*Another time Ed confronted a belligerent young man who was
behaving badly on the course and damaging a tee box. The vandal
challenged him and asked testily, 'Just who the hell do you think
you are?' At the time Edgar was an honorary deputy sheriff and
had a law enforcement ID card that he rarely used, but the young
man's belligerence rattled him, so he pulled out what he thought
was his honorary Sheriff's ID card, but in error he pulled out an ID
card that had been issued as a joke by the sheriff to his dog,
Kenzie, that portrayed Kenzie's photograph and paw print. When
the young man saw the card, he burst out laughing. Realizing he
had flashed the wrong card, Edgar also began laughing and the
young man began behaving like a gentleman.*
— Gary Koeppel

Edgar holding pin and new flag during 2006 Clubhouse renovation.

There are very few real gentlemen anymore. Ed had a significant presence, a confidence and other qualities and he didn't need to attract attention to himself; he was pleased when attention came, but he never sought it. He was satisfied with who he was while always improving himself, and he was comfortable with his personality and his own body. Other people's opinions certainly mattered to him, but he didn't base his life on them.

— Tom Gray

FAIR PLAY

Edgar may have learned the quality of fair play from the ethics of the game of golf, but he tended to apply them to every situation, including matters of money, litigation and poachers on a golf course.

A DAY LATE AND DOLLAR LONG

I was the last member when the club came out with a new plan and reduced membership fees. The next time I saw Nancy Parsons, the membership director, I kidded that I had been a day late and a dollar short, which she apparently told Edgar who replied, 'he means a day early and a dollar long.' A week later I received a check refunding me $8,000. Just like that.

— Jim Heurerman

PRINCIPLE FOR WINNING

If Ed felt he was right about a controversy, he didn't back away from the fight. Of the eight or nine legal matters that led not only to litigation but also to actual trial, we never lost one. That was due as much to Ed's straightforward manner and principled objective as to anything else.

— Myron "Doc" Etienne, Jr., Esq.

THE POACHERS

Often Ed would catch 'golf poachers' who played the course without paying. He'd approach them in his humble style and tell them he'd done the same thing many times when he was young. He said he would not ask them to leave but, after finishing their round, to please come back to the clubhouse and pay for their round by cleaning some carts, bagging balls, raking traps, and so on. This taught them the value of fair play and prevented vandalism by angry poachers who had been kicked off the course.

— Gary Koeppel

A DATE WITH THE RYDER CUP

I loved being on the golf course with my dad. One day he showed up unexpectedly at the high school and took me to the Grill Room in Pebble Beach where the members of the Ryder's Cup were having lunch. I was 17 and the Ryder guys were in their 20s, flirting and talking with British, Scotch and Irish accents. It was something else for me and they got a kick out of talking to an American teenager. That was my dad, for he, he kinda knocked me out with that sort of thing.

— Anne Haber

KINDNESS

With the Habers there seemed to be no "random acts of kindness" because kindness was basic and persuasive.

ORDER GLOVES, PLEASE

Howard Hawkins was a retired member of less than modest means who lived nearby and began doing small things around the course. Mr. Haber never let anyone do anything free for him, so he gave Mr. Hawkins a cart that he used to oversee the entire golf course and repaired pins, ball marks, divots — anything that was damaged, he'd fix. So Mr. Haber would give him passes for dinner at The Covey, a free account in the pro shop, complimentary gas when we had a station on site. They became close friends. One morning Mr. Haber came into the shop one cold January morning and said, 'Howard's out there early every morning and it's cold. He needs some gloves, so please order some in his size.'

— Bonnie Chapman

THREE LITTLE ELEPHANTS

I love elephants, so I was either going to be an elephant trainer or a fireman. In his office Mr. Haber had three teak elephants that had been given to him by a dear friend. In 1977 in a condominium fire I got badly burned. Mr. Haber rushed me to the emergency room and helped save my life. When he came to visit me in the hospital, which was hard for him because he didn't like to see people suffer, he brought me his three elephants and asked me to take care of them for him.

— Sidney Reade

MODESTY / DEFERENCE

Edgar never took credit for his accomplishments; rather, he tended to deflect any recognition or compliments by deferring to others and giving them credit, a characteristic that some have ironically referred to as his worst fault.

DON'T WIND UP LIKE YOUR COUSIN

My cousin Edgar was older but not a very close relative. My mother used to warn me harshly that if I didn't work hard, make good grades and do something with my life, that I would wind up just like my cousin Edgar.

— Charles Haber

DON'T THANK ME

In 1967 I began my medical practice in Carmel Valley and everyone knew Edgar Haber as Chief Quail of Quail Lodge or as Eagle One, a moniker given him after he eagled the first hole at Saint Andrews during an Amateur Open. Everyone in the valley was proud of him and he was the man to know; after all, he created a five-star hotel, started the Mid-Valley Fire Department and cultivated law enforcement officers who kept an eye out for the village. He asked me to be the volunteer physician for the first Carmel Valley Fire Department. He actually made my life as a doctor easier through the years as a first responder and founder of the fire department and the countywide emergency medical response. To me the most interesting thing was that he was so magnanimous. Many times I heard him say, 'Well, don't thank me, thank old so-and-so over there…'

— Paul Tocchet, MD

Edgar Haber with frequent guests Arnold Palmer and Lee Martin

Edgar and Lawson on the signature 17th green.

THE MILITARY MEDAL

Not many people knew Edgar got a medal in WWII. He was stationed somewhere in the South Pacific and was in charge of record keeping for a huge supply warehouse containing billions of tons of war materiel.He calculated the exact contents of his warehouse by counting the number of boxes in each row, then estimating the number of rows and figured, 'Well, that looks like so-and-so many boxes each containing so many items and therefore we had that much stuff.' He never counted the items and he never kept any records. He obtained his medal by virtue of his estimates, but as usual, he never spoke of it.

— Anthony Lombardo, Esq.

MENTORING

Almost every Quail Lodge employee interviewed commented about how much they learned from Edgar Haber. He seemed to have a way of seeing everything and gently correcting both large and small errors made by staff in every department. Their compliments about Mr. Haber the Mentor are too voluminous to include, so only a few are noted here.

KICKSTANDS

I first met Mr. Haber when I was a young girl when he knocked on our door and talked to my folks; he was selling life insurance. It wasn't often in Carmel Valley you would see a very well dressed man, especially one going door to door. As he left he saw that our bicycles were lying down. Assuming they were not well cared for, he told me that he had children at home and said if we didn't want the bicycles he'd be happy to take them off our hands. When I said they were lying on the ground because they didn't have kickstands, and they didn't have kickstands because they were hand-me-down bikes that we rode everyday to school, he said he thought I was very clever for letting him know that we did appreciate our bicycles. And that's how I met him.

— Sidney Reade

THE LESSONS NEVER END

Edgar was the president in name only after he sold Quail Lodge to the Peninsula Hotel Group, but he continued caring and attending to details, large and small. One day as we sat down to lunch, and he began rearranging the silverware. The waiter came over and he said nicely, 'Next time you set up the tables, this is where to put the fork and napkin so it sets an image when someone sits down, a feeling that guests get at the start of their meal' and the waiter thanked him for the lesson.

— Clayton Larson

MY MENTOR LIST

If you were paying attention, nothing Ed Haber did was unintentional except, perhaps, getting on my personal Mentor List. As I grew older I began to appreciate seeing him around the property, which he seemed to be everywhere, all the time, or being cordial to a VIP guest or a grounds keeper, never being above or below anybody, just being the consummate gentleman at all times. He was a walking mentor.

— Ducky O'Toole

Kenzie asking Edgar if he can ride with him in the helicopter.

THE LESSON

Although vandalism was rare, on one occasion Edgar caught four local high school students who had caused some serious damage to the greens. He confronted them and said he wouldn't involve their parents or the sheriff; that they could help after school and weekends to work off the cost to repair the damage. One of the boys eventually became the assistant course superintendent and, the father of another young vandal, a prominent business executive, only many years later learned about his son's vandalism and about Edgar's fairness, so he called and thanked Ed for not making the incident public or for calling the sheriff and, especially, for giving his son such a valuable lesson.

— Gary Koeppel

THE BUTT OF LEADERSHIP

When I got out of the Navy, I practiced on Quail as my home course, then explored playing tournament golf and decided I wasn't good enough, so I returned to Carmel Valley and applied for work at the golf club in 1976. As a golfer on the Carmel High School Team I, of course, knew Mr. Haber, but interviewing for a job to work for him was a different matter. We left his office to take a walk; he said, 'You know, Lawson, working at a golf club is a little different than playing at one,' he said as he was picking up a cigarette butt. As we continued walking, he continued picking up cigarette butts, and I'm wondering if I should pick up the next one, even though I wasn't working there yet. I wound up working for him for the next 30 years, then another six years after he sold the property. So you can imagine how many cigarette butts I picked up during those 36 years at Quail. It was a great lesson in both humility and leadership.

— Lawson Little

BUSINESS IN BOHEMIA

When growing up on the Peninsula, I would go with my dad to a coffee house in Monterey he started, called Sancho Panza, in a walled Spanish building with a courtyard full of flowers that was frequented by bohemians who played chess, read poetry and listened to Jazz. My folks also took me to Big Sur at Nepenthe and Slates Hot Springs, that became Esalen. I believe it was these impressions that inspired me to seek an alternative lifestyle and become an American craftsman earning a living with my hands, all of the business knowledge for which I learned from my father.

— Marilyn Haber

Chief Founder

It's not what you do that counts, it is the great people around you who matter.

— Edgar Haber

CO-FOUNDING A FIRE DEPARTMENT

In the early 1970s the Carmel Valley Volunteer Fire Department provided fire protection to their eastern boundary that was west of what is now Garland Park; the Carmel station of the California Division of Forestry (CDF) was the only fire protection for the rest of the valley, which was inadequate because of the long response time. In addition, CDF's equipment was for wild land, not structural fires and the foresters were not trained for fighting structural fires. Subsequently, the fire insurance rates for homes and businesses were at their highest possible price at the highest rating level, which was an exorbitant "10," which was ultimately reduced to an affordable level "5" after the department was formed.

Several community leaders began discussing how to establish a fire district for a volunteer fire department that was needed to serve the entire community, among whom were Skip Marquard, Mike Tancredi, Steve Thigpen Bill Brown and Edgar Haber. The founding was a collaborative effort for which Edgar served as the project catalyst.

We initially formed a county service area that later became an official fire district. Initially we didn't know how much time, effort and money it would take to do this, but it finally came about in the early 1970s. The largest obstacle we needed to overcome was finding the right piece of real estate in the right area for the right price. It was a tough challenge for Edgar who turned out to be the key part by raising a lot of money at Quail Lodge and by persuading the administrator of the Carmel Valley Manor to donate the land for the fire station that, fortuitously, was perfectly located in the middle of the service area where equipment could roll out in near-equal distances in either direction. Once we had the land the task, still arduous, became much less so.
— *Skip Marquard*

Serendipitously, a young woman who was working at Quail Lodge was asked by Edgar to become secretary during the meetings of the fire department founders at the Clubhouse. When Sidney Reade was a small child, her only two passions were either to become an elephant trainer or a fireman. She had even encouraged her father to become a volunteer fireman at the Carmel Valley department and would often dress up in his turn out gear. She was so passionate about fire fighting she spent many hours in the firehouse after school and on weekends, incessantly asking the firemen questions about everything fire-related.

So as the founding board's secretary, Sidney constantly provided the businessmen with critical information about fire departments, procedures and equipment. As soon as the organization was founded, she became a charter volunteer member of the department and later the first female Fire Chief in the county.

The architect designed a unique feature to the firehouse that had never been done before. In order for transparency for the community to see how and where their tax dollars had gone, he designed the front of the building's fire engine bay doors to be glass from top to bottom so all of the equipment would be visible.

— *Skip Marquard*

HABER'S FIRE ARMY

One late Friday night I was having a friendly beer with a neighbor Alan Richmond. Mr. Haber's name came up and he said there was more to him than golf; that he was very involved in the community, the sheriff and fire departments. About that time the phone rang, he jumped up and put on his fireman's turn out gear and, as he raced out the door enroute to a fire, he called out behind him, 'Sorry, I'm a volunteer in Haber's Fire Army.'

— *Hunter Finnell*

DAD'S FIRE THING

He helped found the Mid-valley fire department. In the evenings he'd go to the meetings and when a call came in he would respond with the red light flashing and siren screaming. Sometimes I'd even ride with him. Instead of a dad, he seemed like a kid, you know, with all that kid excitement we all associate with firemen and fire engines.

— *Anne Haber*

The glass bays were only one of the firehouse innovations. Because most firehouse accidents to both people and equipment came from backing up the engines into the firehouse after a fire, we had the architect design a 'drive through' so the returning engines could enter the firehouse from behind the building and exit from the front of the building, so the engineers never had to back up the equipment.

— *Sidney Reade*

THE VERTIGO TOWER

The fireman who died in the condo fire where I was badly burned was claustrophobic, which probably caused his death. After the fire when I was in the hospital all bandaged up, Mr. Haber asked what we could do; all volunteer firemen had background checks, but nowhere in the county were firemen tested for claustrophobia and vertigo. I said we needed a training fund to make props and create physical tests, which hadn't been done before. He created a Mark Roy Memorial Training Fund, named after the condo fire casualty, and raised money from friends at Quail and from all the cities in the county, then built a portable, three-story tower that could be towed to each fire station so firemen could train and prove they didn't have vertigo or claustrophobia.

— *Sidney Reade*

THE FIREHOUSE WALLPAPER

When Mr. Haber co-founded the Mid-Valley Fire Department, he and Terry decorated the station with wallpaper left over from The Covey restaurant and other donated furniture and décor items, which did not cost the taxpayers a penny. The Habers had the same feeling of pride for the firehouse as they had for the hotel; they made it feel like home for the firemen who took really good care of it. It had that familiar Ed and Terry Haber touch: if you're going to do something, do it right and do it well, or do not do it at all.

— Sidney Reade

COUNTRY CLUB FIRE HOUSE

Did you ever go into the Mid-Valley Fire Department fire station that Mr. Haber put together when it was new? It was like stepping into a country club. A typical fire station has a bunch of cheap beds and ratty furniture with bare walls and ugly lockers. But, boy, Mid-Valley had great beds and classy furniture, a great weight room, and of course they had a new, top-of-the-line brass fire pole and circular metal stairway…and the entire inside was decorated like a home with pictures on the wall.

— Pat Duvall

Late one night in the '60s, while living in the mid-valley area, our kids came into the bedroom shrieking that the neighbor's garage was on fire. By the time the state forestry fire trucks arrived from their station near CHOMP, the garage and three cars were charred remains. Ed Haber was a board member on the Carmel Valley Fire Department, knew we needed protection moved into action by starting an ad hoc committee with a few of us and, by sheer determination, like a dog with a bone, he got signatures, put a measure on the ballot, twisted some arms and got the issue passed to form a Mid-Valley Fire Department.

— Steve Thigpen

Edgar Haber stands among the founders of the Mid-Valley Fire Station

ESTABLISHING PARAMEDIC SERVICES

A fatal accident occurred during a volunteer muster and family barbecue at the Mid-Valley Fire Department that involved fireman Sidney Reade's son whose life may have been saved if the department would have had defibrillation equipment and if the area would have had Paramedic Service staffed with Emergency Medical Technicians (EMT).

Edgar solved the first problem by buying the defibrillator equipment himself, but establishing paramedic services in the area required involvement and permissions from numerous county departments, but once the task was completed the two fire departments in Carmel Valley were the only two in the entire county whose firemen were trained EMTs.

WHY PARAMEDICS?

Well, here's another chapter for which Mr. Haber deserves full credit. We were having a barbecue at the fire station and some kids were pulling on the volleyball net. The net's heavy pipe worked its way out of the ground, then fell and struck my son in the chest. At first we tried CPR on him, but we needed defibrillators that we didn't have, so we rushed him to the hospital, where he died. Everyone was devastated and I told Mr. Haber the county needed paramedics. The emergency room doctors didn't want the liability of us having that upgrade. First he bought defibrillators out of his own pocket, and then raised money to outfit everyone. Soon we had trained and equipped paramedics in the entire county.

— Sidney Reade

NO HEART ATTACK HERE, PLEASE

There was no paramedic in Carmel Valley 20 years ago, or anywhere, except Pacific Grove had one connection and one place in Salinas. But trying to establish a paramedic service took a lot of work, mostly with the help of Edgar's right arm, Nancy Parsons. To promote the program we ran some reverse psychology advertisements that said, 'If you were going to have a heart attack, please have it in Salinas or Pacific Grove, but nowhere else, especially in Carmel Valley.' It took some time but now, paramedic services are county wide and I guess we've saved literally hundreds of lives with paramedics — and still counting — all thanks to Edgar Haber and Nancy Parsons.

— Sheriff Bud Cook, Ret.

ONLY LOCALS MAY STROKE

We tried to get paramedics established in Carmel and Carmel Valley because there was no emergency medical response, but when we talked to people in Carmel, they told me, 'Well, only the tourists are going to use that.' And I said, 'Well, okay, next time somebody is laying on the street, we're going to ask them, well, are you a tourist or do you live here? If you live here, we will take care of you, otherwise, we won't.' Well, they didn't think that was very funny, but we eventually got paramedics county wide.

— Edgar Haber

SHERIFF'S ADVISORY COUNCIL &
SHERIFF'S EMERGENCY ASSISTANCE TEAM
THE FOUNDING

The following brief anecdotes portray the larger story of Edgar's involvement in founding the Sheriff's Advisory Council, which raised funds privately donated to supplement the sheriff department's budget to purchase needed equipment. Later he founded the Sheriff's Emergency Assistance Team that provided volunteers to assist local fire and law enforcement agencies with manpower to perform emergency duties that freed up the professionals to accomplish more important tasks.

MAINTAINING ORDER

Mr. Haber was the president of the Sheriff's Advisory Council (SAC) when we became aware of the need for a citizen Sheriff's Emergency Assistance Team (SEAT) after the 1987 Pebble Beach fire. We learned we didn't have enough manpower to handle ancillary activities, such as crowd management, perimeter control and isolation, traffic control, communication and record-keeping — all of which would allow peace officer personnel to involve themselves wholly with law enforcement functions. Ed Haber shouldered the leadership and raised large sums of money to outfit each volunteer. They trained often and were well prepared for their first major emergency assignment, the 1989 Loma Prieta Earthquake. Everything was chaotic on the scene, but the volunteer, all-citizen SEAT team quickly responded and began evacuating people and clearing entire areas, controlling traffic and all sorts of other tasks — not for a day, but for days on end that wound up for a few weeks. We could not have maintained order without Haber's incredible team.
— Sheriff Capt. Roger Chatterton, Ret.

Both organizations have a rich history of service provided by countless local volunteers through the years. The amount of money raised and number of volunteer services rendered to the local emergency agencies will never be fully accounted for or given proper credit, but then that was never the motivations of those who contributed so much to the community and in so many ways.

The history of these two volunteer organizations is rich and voluminous, but below are few sample accounts of the services rendered by these remarkable organizations and also serve as modest reminders of the value of volunteer community service.

GETTING IT DONE

Regarding public safety, Ed Haber instinctively knew what to do but getting it done was often frustrating. He understood procedures and jurisdiction, but was often thwarted by going through hoop after bureaucratic hoop, which is why he founded the Sheriff's Advisory Council, a fund-raising citizen's group, which was where he was most comfortable and most effective. To get it done, he always did it himself and with like-minded friends.
— James Hill, III

WHERE THERE'S A NEED…

Before the 1987 wildfire in Pebble Beach that burned 36 homes, none of the agencies were equipped for any emergency response. There was no organization, no radios that communicated between the local police with the fire department or the sheriff's office.

They had virtually no inter-department communications, no equipment or system set up. So I got the idea of getting a group together who could raise funds for equipment and serve as citizen volunteers to help the enforcement agencies. By the time the Loma Prieta earthquake occurred, we had a well-trained volunteer group called the Sheriff's Emergency Assistance Team, or SEAT, that provide all kinds of help with evacuations, relocations, property protection, traffic control — things the sheriff shouldn't have to waste trained manpower to do, so we did it for them as volunteers. I must say we did accomplish some pretty good things and by the time of the 6.9 earthquake in 1989, we were ready to serve.

— Edgar Haber

PAYING FORWARD

I spent five years as a volunteer on Edgar's S.E.A.T. team for two reasons. First, in 1970 returning from college in Colorado I was stranded in a snowstorm inside my car for three days before the sheriff finally found us. Second, joining Ed Haber's Sheriff's Emergency Assistance Team was my pay back or, as they say nowadays, my pay forward, for the sheriff rescuing me.

— Robert Talbott, Jr.

THE GOLF SWING AND LAW ENFORCEMENT

In dealing with the SAC and SEAT organizations, Edgar became quite adept at how to be an expert at navigating the personalities, jurisdictions and politics in the world of law enforcement. He once said it was no different than the feel of a golf club. If you take your backswing back too far or swing too fast, you're not going to get the same outcome as with a slow swing with a smooth tempo. I believe that's how he was able to understand and deal with so many kinds of people.

— James Hill, III

FROM UNIFORMS TO TRAILERS

When asked how much money Sheriff's Advisory Counsel raised for the sheriff's office, I replied, 'Well, we had some nice contributors; we raised enough money to buy everything that wasn't in their taxpayer budget, such as portable radios, a trailer command post, that sort of thing, even uniforms.' There were some guys who couldn't afford uniforms, so we saw that they got them but we never told anybody who paid for it, in other words, nobody knew whether you paid for your uniform or if you didn't, and that was something that I thought was a better way to do it because you didn't want to have a guy say, 'Well, you bought him a uniform, and I had to pay for mine,' that would be awful. To answer the question, I think we raised about $750,000 during the first two or three years, money that bought a lot of useful equipment that the sheriff wouldn't have had otherwise, so it all kinda worked out okay.

— Edgar Haber

BY THE S.E.A.T. OF HIS PANTS

During the Pebble Beach fire when he saw deputies directing traffic and other mundane tasks that trained citizens could be doing and freeing the officers for more important duties, he founded the Sheriff's Emergency Assistance Team. He was intuitive the way he could quickly perceive what could or should be done to improve public safety and somehow, often by the seat of his pants, he was able to bring about some amazing things like S.E.A.T.

— James Hill, III

Train lover helps revive Del Monte line

Monterey-S.F. service may begin next July

By Bill Glines
Staff Writer

Ed Haber, the white-haired boss of the posh Quail Lodge and Carmel Valley Golf and Country Club near Monterey, has had a lifelong love affair with rail travel.

His special pet has been the Del Monte, which began service between San Francisco and Monterey in the early 1900s. Southern Pacific killed the passenger service in 1971, saying it was unprofitable.

"I can understand why no one wanted to ride trains back then," Haber said. "Equipment was old and dirty, service was poor and there were 23 stops between here and San Francisco. There never should have been more than five or six."

Now, the train may begin service again by July of next year, and Haber deserves much of the credit.

Haber said the feelings that killed the Del Monte began to change in 1973 when the oil shortage hit. Americans were lining up at gasoline stations, rationing was being discussed and other modes of travel began getting a second look.

Business that summer dropped 25 percent at Monterey Peninsula hotels and restaurants during the Crosby Pro Am Golf Tournament. People had been scared out of their cars, and there was no rail service to get golf fans to Pebble Beach.

On Dec. 15 that year, Haber called a meeting that included promoters whose events depended largely on spectators who came from outside the area. The events included the annual Bach Festival, Monterey County Symphony concerts, Laguna Seca auto races, Pacific Grove Butterfly Festival, the Crosby, Clint Eastwood Tennis Tournament and the Monterey Jazz Festival.

Also attending were city officials from Carmel, Seaside, Pacific Grove and Monterey and officials from the Sierra Club; Fort Ord; the U.S. Naval Postgraduate School; restaurant, motel and motel associations; chambers of commerce; and taxpayer associations.

At this meeting, Haber, a persuasive insurance man before heading the Carmel Valley venture, drove home the message that the economy of the Monterey Peninsula depended a great deal on passenger rail connections with the rest of California.

A special guest at the meeting was Eddie Elkins, a longtime porter on the Del Monte club car. On the morning trip north out of Monterey, it was Elkins who had squeezed the orange juice and poured it into glasses, fixed the raisin toast and served the coffee. Late in the afternoon on the return trip from San Francisco, Elkins served the martinis and snacks with great aplomb.

"He got a standing ovation," Haber said. "You should have seen him beam. Most of us who rode the Del Monte regularly remembered Eddie."

Haber, who is in his late 60s and has the ruddy cheeks of a man who still plays a good game of golf, began riding the Del Monte in the early 1930s when he lived in San Francisco, where he grew up and was a city champion. He made the rail trip annually to compete in the California State Golf Championship, which then was played at Pebble Beach.

Haber's next major step was to distribute 7,500 "Great Train" quizzes, and 2,388 Monterey Peninsula residents said they would ride the Del Monte if service were restored. An additional 137 said they wouldn't.

Bill Glines — Mercury
Ed Haber rode the Del Monte in the '30s when he lived in San Francisco

Nearly half of those favoring the service said they would commute between Monterey and San Francisco at least four times a year.

Shopping and visiting friends were listed as major reasons for going to San Francisco by 1,751 respondents. A total of 1,561 checked the box that said they would ride the train "to avoid using my auto." About 1,700 said they would prefer to ride in a parlor, or club, car where refreshments are served.

Armed with these replies, Haber began beating the drums for a renewed Del Monte. He began gaining the interest of citizens in towns along the route that had had the service, including Gilroy, Morgan Hill, San Jose, Palo Alto, Burlingame and San Francisco.

The key that turned the lock on the project was an appropriation in the past year by the state Legislature of $2.5 million to pay costs of getting tracks replaced where they had been torn out and extending Southern Pacific service in San Francisco through the Financial District to the Ferry Building.

But before the legislation was approved and signed by Gov. Edmund G. Brown Jr., it had been necessary to enlist the support of Adriana Giancturco, who heads the state Department of Transportation; state Sens. Al Alquist, D-San Jose, and Henry Mello, D-Monterey; and Assemblyman Sam Farr, D-Monterey.

The toughest part was bringing together Giantur-

co, who has run her department with an iron hand, and Alquist. The two have quarreled publicly for many years over highway appropriations. Alquist once introduced legislation that would have halted payment of Gianturco's salary.

Haber recalls the day a call came to him in Carmel Valley from Gianturco. She announced interest in seeing the Del Monte back on the tracks and wondered whether Haber would do some friendly lobbying for money to get the project started.

Haber quickly arranged for the two old antagonists — Alquist and Gianturco — to meet in Sacramento at a neutral site: Mello's office. Not long after the meeting, Alquist, Farr and Mello began carrying the legislation for the $2.5 million appropriation.

In discussing his part in the effort to revive the Del Monte, Haber quickly disclaimed credit.

"People up and down the line did it," he said. "People like Mayor Gerald Fry in Monterey and Bill Paterson, a school trustee in Gilroy. I was simply the catalyst."

He predicted that the day is coming soon when rail travel again will move many Americans from place to place.

"There's going to be another oil shortage," he said. "Rail travel is already of major importance in Japan and Europe. The Los Angeles-to-San Diego commute started with a single train a few years ago. Now there are eight trains a day."

BRING BACK THE DEL MONTE EXPRESS

I first met Edgar in 1978 when I was publishing the Big Sur Gazette newspaper. I learned that a man in Carmel Valley had started a campaign to "Bring Back the Del Monte Express," the original steam locomotive rail service between San Francisco and Monterey. At the time, the country was suffering from gas shortages and the peninsula tourism was hit hard by the decrease in tourism. His idea was to revive the train service so visitors could come to the peninsula without a gasoline vehicle, then be greeted by vans from the various hotels, and given a rental car with a tank of gas to tour around the peninsula. The rail service would have relieved some of the tourism problems caused by the oil embargo. I interviewed Edgar and ran a four-page feature article about his efforts, which were extensive, although in the end politics prevailed in Sacramento and Southern Pacific Railroad scuttled the legislation because they owned Greyhound Bus Lines and preferred freight rather than passenger service. During this encounter we realized our common interests: we both published newspapers, founded fire departments and served our communities; an introduction that evolved into a close friendship that lasted for the next 27 years.

— Gary Koeppel

Chief Responder

When my car turned over on Tehama Road, I was hanging upside down when the deputy arrived. I told him to be sure to report that I was the first person on the scene.

— Edgar Haber

Many who knew Edgar Haber knew that he was a frustrated fireman and policeman, which was probably true given his penchant for community service and personal involvement.

The San Francisco earthquake and fire occurred six years before his birth, but his parents' stories of the event must have made a strong impression on him because it destroyed their home, caused them to live in a tent in Golden Gate Park for awhile and was the reason they ferried to the East Bay where they lived after the fire.

Not long after arriving in Carmel Valley during the 1950s, Edgar became a director of the Carmel Valley Fire Department. After building Quail Lodge and realizing that fire department's response time to mid-valley was too distant, with other community leaders, he founded the Mid-Valley Fire Department and, according to Skip Marquard, was the catalyst in its formation because he arranged for the donation of the land where the firehouse was to be built, which was fortuitously mid-way east and west of the fire district.

Regarding law enforcement, soon after acquiring the Morrow Dairy Farm, the future home of Quail Lodge Golf and Country Club, he began numerous life-long relationships with Monterey County sheriffs and deputies, officers and members of the California Highway Patrol, and the representative of the local Federal Bureau of Investigation.

Admittedly some of his interests in the Mid-Valley Fire Department were to reduce the insurance rate for Quail Lodge, as well as for other area businesses and residents. Likewise, his interest in law enforcement was both in providing security for Quail Lodge and its guests and for the Carmel Valley community at large. As with most of his involvements, his motivations were both personal and community: they were "win-win."

He is perhaps best remembered as a civilian with an official Monterey County Sheriff's red light, siren and police radios on his private Mercedes vehicle, which a few law enforcement officers as well as community members resented.

Why does a private citizen have all of this official equipment and why does he respond like a fireman or policeman to a fire or law enforcement incident in Carmel Valley?

MERCEDES WITH A RED LIGHT

I never knew Ed to be a braggart or boast about his successes, but he did enjoy the nicer things in life. One was his Mercedes station wagon. It was a custom-painted, two-tone black and gold color. He outfitted it as a first responder vehicle. It had a police radio, removable revolving red light, and emergency equipment box in the back that included the usual array of gadgets. He had a concealed weapon permit and would carry as circumstances dictated. Now, that was a sight to see — a Mercedes rolling to the scene of call with red light whirling. It almost looked like a scene from a movie. He loved it all.
— Sheriff Bud Cook, Ret.

THE BLACK AND GOLD

When he got his new gold and black Mercedes, in which he just had all the police equipment installed, you know, top of the line, he gets me in the car and he's got to drive me all around in this thing, showing me how all the equipment worked, turning on the siren, the whole program, the whole show and tell, and acting just like a kid getting a new toy. Ed had an uncanny ability to integrate his passions with his vocations, like the kid playing with toys and the man creating a golf course and hotel.
— Tom Gray

Numerous law enforcement and fire department personnel commented in the interview that, while a few resented his actions, most were appreciative of his "First Responder" actions because he never overstepped his role as a citizen volunteer and because he was extremely helpful in emergency situations and saved many lives by his fast response that usually preceded the official responders.

This chapter could have taken up the space of an entire book, but the selected anecdotes herein from numerous officers and officials portray the essence of his efforts.

WITH RED LIGHT A'BLAZIN'
I was often in his office when his police scanner would go off. He'd reach into his drawer, grab his gun and strap it on, then grab his yellow jacket off the rack, head for his Mercedes and fly down the road with red light a'blazin.' He was a character, quite a character.
— Don Chapin

THE NOT-SO WANNABE
A few law enforcement people resented Edgar for being a first responder and assistant deputy sheriff, but most regarded him as a strong asset for the force and community. He may have been a frustrated, wannabe cop deep down, but knew he wasn't a cop, so he did the next best thing by supporting law enforcement in more ways than any sheriff can. He did everything from being a first responder to every possible kind of emergency throughout the valley — and, never overstepped his role — to actually founding a fire department, county-wide paramedic services, a Sheriff's Advisory Committee (SAC) and a Sheriffs Emergency Assistance Team (S.E.A.T.). He volunteered thousands of hours of his time and raised literally hundreds of thousands of dollars to support the organizations he founded.
— Sheriff Mike Kanalakis, Ret.

THE CARROT, NOT THE STICK
Haber was very pro law and order, but his heart was more in service than enforcement. One day our deputies caught some kids who'd stolen some golf carts and tore up some greens badly. After talking with the kids and their parents, Ed said, 'You know, I'm convinced these kids won't ever do this again. They worked off their damages doing odd jobs. One of them became a very successful, decorated JAG attorney in Afghanistan and is now an assistant DA in Monterey County. So I guess he had the right touch.
— Sheriff Mike Kanalakis, Ret.

BAYONET ON THE BEACH

In those days I was singing at a lot of weddings and I had permission to use my lunch hour to sing in a wedding at the Catholic mission. I kept a white robe in my trunk in case I was on duty and I had to sing in a wedding. I'm out singing "Ave Maria" by Bach and the dispatcher says there's a guy wielding a bayonet over on the State Beach. As I finished singing, just like Superman, I tossed of my robe and strapped on my holster and, sure enough, when I got to the beach, this guy's holding about 50 people at bay who had been enjoying a picnic. He's callin' me a black SOB and waving that bayonet at me; I didn't have a back up and was afraid I'd have to shoot him, but just then Edgar showed up and got the drop on him with his .38, so we cuffed him and took him to the slammer. I was so relieved I gave Ed a hug, which kinda surprised him, and said, 'Every time I look around, you're always here.'

— Pat DuVall

A VAMP IN A BLOOD BANK

Those days the sheriff's office was short on deputies and I was patrolling alone most of the time, so I was as happy as a vampire in a blood bank to have Mr. Haber around to back me up from time to time. Even when there were accidents on the valley road, he usually got to the scene even before the Highway Patrol did.

— Pat DuVall

CATCHING A 19 AT 69

One afternoon I was patrolling in the village and the call came in about a guy in a Volkswagen bus hit that fence where Clint Eastwood's place used to be. The guy had hit the fence and he was out cold on the ground. So I'm driving Code 3 from the village while Ed heard the call and was already there, getting a blanket to cover the guy when, all of a sudden the kid took off running because he had some outstanding warrants. Ed was 69 then and the kid was 19, but Ed chased him from the Road to the river and hauled him back. I looked at that guy and I said, 'You ain't worth a plug nickel. Here you are, a young punk and you let this old gentleman catch you and bring you back. Serves you right.'

— Pat DuVall

CODE 3 TO CHOMP

The 1997 condo fire at Quail was devastating. One fireman died and I had severe third-degree burns all over my body. When Mr. Haber arrived he quickly sized up the scene. He saw that our only ambulance was being used for the fireman who eventually died. Mr. Haber quickly picked me up and gently put me in his Mercedes, and then rushed me Code 3 to the burn unit at the Community Hospital seven miles away. Enroute, with siren and red light flashing, Mr. Haber radioed ahead to alert the emergency room's burn unit to be prepared for me. When we pulled up he rushed in to bring out the waiting burn team, who took me from there. I had second-degree and third-degree burns on 45 percent of my body and went through 11 surgeries. His actions saved my life.

— Sidney Reade

THE NOT-SO GREAT DANE

Well, you know how we black folks don't take to dogs, especially big ones, but one morning about 4:00 there was a complaint about a great dane chewing up everybody's newspaper. It was real dark and at first I thought it was some kind of four-legged monster, but I got out of the car and, whoa, here comes that dog; it was a good thing I'd left the window down so I jumped through it inside and then that dog was poking his head right in the window and barking something ferocious like. Near scared me to death, then Edgar showed up, talked to the dog real nice and quiet like, and settled him down. Damn. He was there for me again!

— Pat DuVall

LET IT BE SO REPORTED

One evening after dinner with Clint Eastwood and friends at Tehama Golf Club in the hills north of Quail Lodge, as Edgar was driving home on the winding road, his right front wheel caught a 'drainage protrusion,' as he later called it, jutting from the edge of the pavement and, in a split second, his vehicle flipped completely over. Fortunately when the 911 call came over the sheriff's radio, a deputy was nearby on Carmel Valley Road and quickly drove to the scene where he found Edgar hanging upside down from his seatbelt in the vehicle. As the deputy approached, Edgar called out through the open window, 'Officer, let your report show that I was the first person on the scene!'

— Gary Koeppel

LEADERSHIP

WHITE FOLK DON'T TALK TO BLACK FOLK

I grew up in the segregated south and I didn't feel comfortable around white people. At home, when growing up, the old folks said never tell a white man your business. They tell you, 'you see a white man walking and he's grinning, don't trust him.' Those old folks, the sons and daughters of slaves, tell you all kinds of stuff. When I became a Monterey Sheriff Deputy, my first assignment was Carmel Valley and I got to know Mr. Haber pretty well. He'd always go out of his way around anyone and talk with me. Once I confided that I felt bad because I hadn't finished college and Ed told me he hadn't either and said he had quit high school. I felt all right after that. I can't tell you in words how good that felt inside me. Still does. That's the way Ed was.

— Pat DuVall

MR. EASY

Edgar always felt a need for helping his fellow man. I believe his involvement with the fire department was to provide a more efficient, timely and well-equipped service to his local friends, businesses and neighbors. He maintained his down-to-earth, folksy and friendly ways in his daily life. Ed was a person who could move up and down the social ladder with ease. He was comfortable with rich, elite and powerful folks as well as the everyday employee, gardener, waiter and cop on the beat.

— Bud Cook, former Monterey County Sheriff

TRAINING

CONCEALED CARRY

Carmel Valley was still a little wild in those early days of Quail Lodge and some drug use came into the area, nobody had gates and deputies were not always around, so Edgar decided to get a carry concealed permit (CCW) from the sheriff's office. But unlike most applicants who register only one weapon, no, Edgar being Edgar, as one who never did anything part way, actually registered for five firearms on the same permit, a 25 caliber, 32 caliber, 9mm short, a 9mm regular and 45 caliber. Most sheriff deputies only had one or at the most two registered carry permits. To this day deputies still talk about the dude in the valley who had a permit for five revolvers in one card.

— Steve Gould

COURTESIES

THE SPEEDING TICKET

My wife and I were on a road trip in Southern California about 300 miles south of Carmel Valley. A Highway Patrolman pulled me over for speeding. When I showed him my driver's license, he asked if I was related to Edgar Haber of Carmel Valley. Not knowing what to expect, I told him I was his cousin. The officer politely returned my license and said, 'It's a pleasure to meet you Mr. Haber. Please drive carefully and enjoy your trip.'

— Charles Haber

TRADING SKILLS

PINGS FOR PISTOLS

When I started competitive shooting and won the 'Governor's Twenty,' the sheriff wanted to send me to the nationals, but the department had no funds, so Ed and some others donated some money. Later, after returning, I took him out to the range for some shooting and we wound up swapping a set of Ping clubs for a Smith and Wesson pistol. Those were the best clubs at the time and the pistol was hard to come by, so it was a great trade.

— Paul Keane

GOLFING FOR GUNS

Every year our department hosted a Peace Officers Association pistol match and many of the guys wanted to play golf while here, so of course, every year they wound up playing golf at Quail. For some reason, the next time I saw Ed, he'd always have two or three new guns and probably two or three fewer sets of golf clubs.

— Paul Keane

A Gentleman's Game

At least 93% of the putts you leave short will not go in.

— *Edgar Haber*

Every golfer understands the great lessons of life offered by the game of golf, such as: enjoying golf as a game despite the many tricks it plays on you; forgiving one's own mistakes, knowing that many if not most are beyond your control; recognizing that learning is a constant because as soon as you learn and master one thing, you forget everything you learned about something else; that honesty on a golf course defines integrity and gains respect from your fellows; knowing that taking risks may or may not be rewarding, and the rewards don't always match the risk; and believing in yourself is challenged with every shot and the better the shot the more faith you have when taking the next one.

Edgar regarded the golf course as a playground to enjoy the greatest game ever invented, a gentleman's game, indeed.

GAME ANYONE?

Mr. Haber enjoyed golf so much he wanted everyone else to enjoy it also. Even if they were just walking by, he would ask if they played golf, and a conversation would begin. His real love was not making money; it was golfing and talking golf — to anyone, anytime. He wanted everyone to play golf. He hosted tournaments, even invited strangers to play. He asked the members to bring in their old golf stuff that we'd sell it in the pro shop to raise money for the Junior Golf program he had started.

— Mary Bayless

A GENTLEMAN'S GAME

Golf has been fortunate to count Ed Haber as among its ambassadors. From his storied amateur career to his significant role in bringing golf to Carmel Valley, he has been a great friend to the game. It's not surprising that golf continues to be an important part of his life. Topping the short list of 'good things about getting older' is the fact that at least it becomes easier for us to shoot our age.

— Jack Nicklaus

SINGLES ALWAYS PLAY

Whenever Edgar began a round, if there was single on the driving range, he always invited him to play.

— Myron "Doc" Etienne, Jr., Esq.

Edgar Haber honored for life in golf

Quail Lodge course creator still active in game at age 89

By ED VYEDA
Herald Staff Writer

When Edgar Haber moved from San Francisco to Carmel Valley in 1946, he didn't have a job. But he settled in anyway. "It was a great place to play golf," he reasoned.

Haber made it even greater, creating the first golf course in the valley at Quail Lodge in 1962 and dedicating his life to the game.

"He is one of the real champions of the game and what it stands for," Carmel Valley's Ron Read, the United States Golf Association Western Region director, said Friday.

The USGA honored Haber with a surprise luncheon at Quail Lodge, where he was presented with a Lifetime Achievement Award by the USGA Volunteers Committee.

"Thank you very much. When do we eat?" Haber quipped upon receiving the plaque from USGA committee member Marsha Juergens of Pebble Beach. "I thought I was just coming here for lunch."

The guest of honor, who turns 89 in July, was applauded for his devotion to the game, which began when he first played in 1929 as a boy. He was skilled enough to win the San Francisco City Championship, and remains active on and off the course.

"He saved the state women's

CLAY PETERSON/Special to The Herald
Edgar Haber, 89, receives an award from Marcia Juergens of the U.S. Golf Association for his years of support for amateur golf.

amateur," Juergens said of Haber. "When the tournament was moved out of Pebble Beach, "he was the one who made Quail Lodge the home of the championship."

Before becoming a golf course developer, Haber was first publisher of the Carmel Valley News, which was printed on an old-fashion mimeograph machine. "I used to feed the paper in one sheet at a time," Haber recalls.

Those were the days when Haber might sneak onto the Pebble Beach Golf Links now and then. "I would play there three times a week — but never saw the first two holes," he

said.

Haber advanced to the quarterfinals of the State Amateur one year, playing in an era when the entry fee was $5 to play Pebble Beach and Cypress Point.

Those are only a few of his fond memories in a game that has shaped his life as much as he helped shape the valley.

"Everything I have done in my life has been because of golf," he said. "Every job I have ever had was because of golf. That's why I came here and that is why I have stayed here."

Still a twice-a-week golfer, Haber

said being honored by the USGA was particularly special. "The USGA stands for integrity and sportsmanship in the game — all the good stuff," he said.

Once he had the idea to build the Quail Lodge golf course on what was once a dairy farm, he found "four or five guys to put up $10,000 each for the down payment."

He is proud of how Quail Lodge has matured over the years, but even more proud of his family, particularly granddaughter Marilyn Beck of Los Angles, who was on hand Friday. "She's in the Peace Corps," Haber was quick to point out.

Her dedication to others must run in the genes. Haber has been involved in countless local charities, from the Heart Association to local fire and police department work. He is still a uniformed volunteer for the sheriff's department Emergency Assistance Team.

"He has been a successful and dedicated member of this community," Read said. "You can't name a charity that Ed Haber hasn't been part of in some way.

In Haber's honor, Read is heading up a foursome that is to include his son, Ryan Read, to play 89 holes at Quail Lodge on July 22 — Haber's birthday — in an effort to raise money for Beacon House in Pacific Grove.

"That seems to be fitting for someone like him," Read said.

"I've enjoyed more than 70 years in this game," Haber said. "I hope I can enjoy another 70."

THE UN-CASHED CHECK

At the end of my interview with Ed Haber for membership in Quail, we compared handicaps and he reminded me of a house rule that he never lost a match to a new member. He was 86 at the time and I was 65 and he asked me to join him Friday because his group could use a young fellow like me. A week later on the first hole I got, for me, a rare birdie. He was quiet as we returned to the cart, and then he said with a straight face, 'You know, we haven't cashed your check yet.'

— Sam Trust

GOLF FOR THE NEW GUY

As a new deputy I had the night shift on patrol in the Valley. Around dawn, when it was slow, I'd scrounge some day-old bread from the Safeway dumpster and take it to the lakes at Quail to feed the ducks. Early one morning this guy came around, we just talked for a while, and he asked if I golfed. I was only a duffer but he wrote on a card, 'Golf for Two. Ed.' One day I showed the card to Bob Holmes, the pro in the golf shop, who just said, 'Okay, just get a cart and go.'

— Paul Keane

PLEASE CLEAN OUT YOUR LOCKER

Edgar was a fast but polite and gentlemanly golfer. One day, a new member playing with a group in front of him was playing very slowly. Time after time the slow player did not let the faster group play through. Finally, at the 9th, Edgar went ahead and asked to play through, but instead of apologizing, the new member responded rudely, 'I am a member and have the same rights as you do,' whereupon Edgar excused himself from his group and left the course. When the slow play member arrived on the 18th green, Edgar handed him a check with a letter cancelling his membership and asked him politely to clean out his locker. It was said this was the only time this ever happened.

— William A. Anderson, Pebble Beach

YOU OWE ME FIVE

Ed's wit was as dry as his memory was long. When he was 90 he birdied 13 with a seven iron off the green and won the skins. I left the game early and was short of funds so I said I'd pay him later. When we went to his 91st Birthday, he was shaking hands with everyone as they entered his home, but as I walked in he said, 'you owe me five bucks.'

— Sam Trust

THE OLD COURSE

A REAL GENT

During the 1963 British Amateur Championship tournament at the Old Course at St. Andrews, the Scottish Daily Express reported that well-known caddie, John Abernethy, sacked the American Walker Cup star, Richard Sikes, because the golfer had refused to pay his lunch money. 'Americans have huge bags, make heavy divots and are difficult to look after. Sikes paid me only one pound for each of two rounds.' The next day he carried for the California amateur, Edgar Haber, and said, 'now I've got a yank that's a real gent.'

— Express Staff Reporter

A GOOD HOLE, NOT A GREAT HOLE

Edgar played the Old Course at St. Andrews several times, a few during British Amateur Opens. As a member of the RNA I invited him there to play. He said he'd already been there and played. Everyone who knew him knew on the first hole after his drive he had knocked in his nine-iron shot for an eagle, which is where he got his Eagle nickname. When I asked how he like the first hole, he said, 'Well, it was a good hole, not a great hole, and I've been there, so I don't need to do it again.'

— Ron Reed

THE CYCLE OF THE GAME

Jim Langley was the golf pro at Cypress Point for 34 years. After losing one arm in an accident, he learned how to play golf with only his left arm and played so well he left most of his competitors trailing behind him. He was only the second golfer ever granted an honorary membership at Cypress Point; the first was Dwight D. Eisenhower, the 34th president.

Well, perhaps I have an experience with Ed Haber unique to anyone else. In 1964, before I turned pro, I had gotten to the final round of the President's flight and was matched with Mr. Haber. I was 26 and he was about 59. It was a great match, but I'd been honing my game at the Q School and barely squeaked by to win the match. That's how we met. Through the years we played on and off many times, either at Quail or Cypress. It may sound strange to say, but somehow our hearts were intertwined without saying so. We always responded to each other and shared thoughts, whether about golf or a community issue like the water problem. You might say, we went through the cycle of the game together.

— Jim Langley

As a member of Cypress, Edgar was often my guest and he probably played more rounds than I did. When the suitors from Hong Kong were considering purchasing Quail, they loved to play golf and Edgar would make a big deal out of getting them on Cypress, knowing that all he had to do was give me a call.

— Bob Shepard

CYPRESS IS NICE, BUT HOW DO YOU GET ON QUAIL?
Edgar's birthdays were special affairs and his friends often got creative about his celebrations, though he always asked for pet food as presents that he donated to the SPCA. In 1997 on his 85th birthday, I had a different idea for a gift I thought he might enjoy. I telephoned my friend, Bill Bates, the witty Carmel cartoonist, and asked him to draw three golfers on a green surrounded by Cypress trees on the edge of the ocean with the caption, 'Cypress Is Nice, But How Do You Get On Quail?' The framed original cartoon was presented to him at lunch along with a copy of that day's Friday edition of the Carmel Pine Cone, which featured the same cartoon. Edgar was not known to display congratulatory plaques on his office wall, but he hung the cartoon in a special place were he could enjoy it from his desk.
— *Gary Koeppel*

THE 12th AT CYPRESS
On day after lunch in the dining room at Cypress Point when Edgar was 91, we got in a golf cart and he asked to stop at the 12th tee. He said, 'I've a memory of this hole, not a very good one, but during a state amateur tournament I was leading after the first day. On the second, I hit my driver into the bunker and didn't get out as well as I should have and bogeyed the hole, which cost me the tournament.'
— *Clayton Larson*

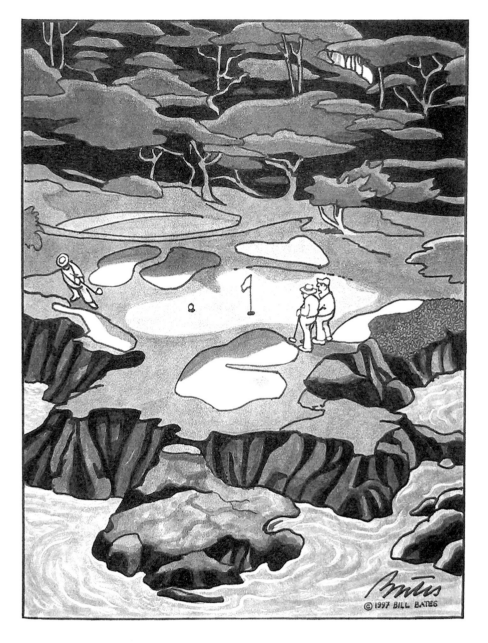

"Cypress is nice, but how do you get on Quail?"

POACHING PEBBLE

CART ENVY

My Japanese friend Micheo Inakage was a close friend of Hiroshi Watanabe, the president of the Lone Cypress Company that owned Pebble Beach at the time. During one of the most miserable rounds of golf in my life, as we came in on 18 we were fully drenched and freezing cold, largely because the carts had no roofs. When we got into the Tap Room I happened to mention in conversation that I was a member at Quail and, although it rarely rained in Carmel Valley, when it did we had carts with roofs on them and stayed dry. It took only two weeks before Pebble was equipped with new carts that had roofs on them.

— Gary Koeppel

PARKING AT PEBBLE

You know you always want to stretch your resources. This is the one. And word of mouth is great promotion, as it was necessary to get people here on a low-to-no budget. So during one of the Crosby Clambake tournaments, he would take his black and gold station wagon with 'Carmel Valley Golf and Country Club' painted boldly on the doors, park it right in front of the entrance to the Pebble Beach Lodge, and walk away with the keys in his pocket. He left it there all week where thousands of people saw this tasteful but obvious advertisement in the most prominent place on the property where nobody could miss seeing it. All week. The front desk would call him, 'Ah, Mr. Haber, your car is here in the front…,' and he'd say, 'yeah, the fuel pump blew and we're waiting for a part, you know, or some such thing.'

— Lawson Little

THE ONLY MEMBER OF PEBBLE BEACH

Mr. Haber had an entrepreneurial spirit and was always thinking about how to improve his business. He structured a deal with Pebble Beach. They were also eager to increase play. If you were a member of the Beach Club you were also a member of Quail and vice versa, so they issued reciprocity certificates and it worked very well. But, in later years those special memberships were revoked because SFB Morse's last will and testament had decreed Pebble Beach would always be a public and never a private course. However, one member refused to give up her 'membership.' Her husband has been the CEO of the New York Stock Exchange and had built a home on the 14th tee. Every day she'd get in her golf cart and, respectful of other play, she would start somewhere on the course and play four or five holes. The company could not stop her from exercising a membership that she refused to give up. Few people ever knew that Edgar created the only memberships Pebble Beach Golf Course ever had.

— Laird Small

UNPAID GREEN FEES

Once I invited Hiroshi Watanabe, the president of the Lone Cypress Company, former owner of the Pebble Beach Company, to play a round of golf at Quail with Edgar Haber. During the round Edgar told many stories about how he had played hundreds of rounds at Pebble without ever paying a greens fee. As we sat down in the bar at the 19th, in a face without expression, with tongue-in-cheek, Mr. Watanabe said, 'Mr. Haber, from the information you provided during the round, I have calculated that, exclusive of interest, you are currently indebted to the Pebble Beach Company for unpaid green fees in the approximate amount of $63,780.' For only a split second Edgar did a double-take, then we all burst out in laughter.

— Gary Koeppel

WHY THE CROSBY IN WINTER?

Once during the annual AT&T golf tournament, which had previously been the famous Crosby Clambake tournament, on a cold and wet day in January while riding in the cart trying to keep warm between shots, I asked Edgar why in the world would anyone ever schedule a golf tournament in the worst weather month of the year? Edgar replied, 'Once I asked Bing Crosby the same question and he said, where else and at what other time of year can you have the greatest golfers play the greatest golf courses…under the worst of all possible conditions?'

— Gary Koeppel

UNITED STATES GOLF ASSOCIATION

1894

This Certificate is respectfully presented to

EDGAR HABER

For his many years of Support to Amateur Golf

His participation and patronage to The Great Game of Golf

Is acknowledged and appreciated by the Northern California Committee Members of the United States Golf Association

CALLING THE SHOTS

I must also cite Edgar's exceptionally valuable suggestions in my ongoing book about the Official Exceptions to the Rules of Golf, including Ball Renounced in Flight, Ball Missing in Fairway but Obviously Not Lost, Temporary Restraint of Improper Foliage, Ground Under Protest and Ball in Hand Worth Two or More in Bush.

— Henry Beard, author

BOTANICAL OBSTRUCTION

One day during a round Edgar's ball landed at the base of an enormous bush, blocking a swing in any direction, at which and with a straight face he declared, 'Botanical obstruction, requesting relief,' which he used often after humor author and golfer Henry Beard had coined the expression.

— Gary Koeppel

IT BEATS A HIGH ONE

My golf was never as good as my tennis game, so often my drive would go very high but not very far, like in baseball a high pop up to the pitcher, and as Edgar walked away from the tee box he would comment, 'It beats a high one.' And another of his many one-liners, he's now 85 years old and we're 250 yards from the pin, he looked at me deadly seriously and asked, 'Are they off the green?'

— Ralph Drumheller, Quail Tennis Pro

Edgar Haber qualifying for the 1972 US Open.

BIG SHOTS, LITTLE SHOTS

He often conducted business with a big shot over lunch and then played golf with the same important fellow that afternoon, but he never conducted business as such on the golf course. Golf was guy's time, whether you had a dime or a dollar, everyone was equal, except he always negotiated for his strokes.

— Ralph Drumheller

THE 'UH-OH' SHOT

First on anyone's inventory of Edgar's golf bag of tricks is his mastery of the legendary 'uh-oh' shot, when a skillfully skulled iron shot tracked like a laser straight at the pin from 140 yards out. We stand mesmerized as we observe the subtle, surprisingly graceful stroke with the club that produces the sharp metallic 'whenng' that gives the lethal blade its awesome power, and we marvel at the patently insincere expression of regret that Edgar invariable utters in a low, plaintive, and utterly unconvincing moan as the ball stumbles and staggers directly into the hole.

— Henry Beard, author

BETTER A DOC THAN A GOLFER

Ed knew I was not a great golfer, but every year in appreciation for my emergency medical services in the valley he gave me a complimentary golf membership card. I was too busy to golf much in those days so he'd phone me once in awhile and ask why I wasn't using my membership at the club. One day during a round, while showing me how to hit nine-iron shots just off the green, after far too many poor attempts, I expressed my dismay, but as if to console me, he quipped, 'Well, you're my doctor and I'm sure glad you're a better doc than a golfer.'

— Paul Tocchet, MD

SHOW OFF

In 1958 during one of our many $2.50 rounds of golf at Pebble, at the 12th tee a group of ladies let us play through. Edgar hit a hole-in-one and I called him a 'show off.' Then, 40 years later — to the day, in the mail he sent me a copy of the scorecard for that round with a note, 'Sorry there are not any ladies around.'

— Norman Habermann

POSITIONING THE CART

And while it may seem a minor innovation by comparison, surely anyone who has fallen victim to possible the greatest cart artist the links have ever known, simply falls silent with admiration as he realizes that Edgar has once again managed to place the cart in a position which, while not actually blocking his opponent's swing, it reduced the clearance between the club head at full extension and the metal roof support of the strategically placed vehicle into a somewhat nerve-wracking 1/32nd of an inch.

— Henry Beard, author

POACHERS WORK FREE

I had sneaked on the course one day when I was 12 and was approached by Mr. Haber, who knew I wasn't a member, but instead of kicking me out, he said, 'Rake the traps, fix as many ball marks as you can find, play fast and hit it straight.' Later he hired and paid me to take care of things like cleaning the carts and the members clubs. From then on I was able to play nine holes without either paying or sneaking on. Eleven years later I had saved enough to pay for my entire undergraduate college education.

— Tim Blakeslee, Santa Cruz Medical Foundation

KID CADDY CASH

I used to caddy for my dad sometimes when he played at Pebble. I was too young to carry a bag so I pulled a cart. And he would pay me a base pay of a buck fifty or so, and if he got a par I got another 25 cents and 50 cents for a birdie. So the better his game, the more I made. I learned where to stand and what to do and what not to do, I counted up all the pars and all the birdies and did pretty well for a 10-year-old. But he wouldn't let me caddy for nothing; he always insisted on paying me for helping, though I'm pretty sure I was not much help.

— Warren Haber

LOOK WHO'S HERE

We never knew who was going to show up for the Friday afternoon games. I was looking for a regular game until being introduced to Clint Eastwood as my partner who rode in my cart. I really tried to be cool and play well, neither of which I pulled off, especially on the 18th green when I putted the ball completely off the green. But he was a regular guy and we had some good laughs.

— Ralph Drumheller

THE NEXT FAIRWAY

I always enjoyed walking to the next tee with Edgar and looking to see where the next fairway would take us.

— Lawson Little

THERE'S HOPE FOR CLINT

During a round with Eastwood, Clint said 'You're a great hitter for your age, Ed, and that gives me great hope that I don't have to worry about getting older.'

— Clint Eastwood

BETTER GOLF THAN GREY

I regret not accepting Edgar's offer to be Quail's in-house legal counsel. Had I done so, my hair would not be as grey and my golf game would probably be much better.

— Anthony L. Lombardo, Esq.

Golf Shots, Long

*Twice I gambled my job
with the pros in the shop,
Laird Small and Bob
Holmes, and twice I lost
the bet, so I had to trade
offices for a day.*

— Edgar Haber

Good humor needs no editing and no introduction.

MATCHES

BETTING THE FARM

When I was the golf director at Quail Lodge we called Mr. Haber 'Eagle' because he had eagled the first hole at St. Andrews during one of the British Opens. We'd often play nine holes in the late afternoon and the usual bet was for Quail Lodge — winner takes all. It took awhile but the first time I won I left his secretary Nancy a note that I was the new owner. The next morning the Eagle arrived at his office to find my name on his door with a note listing his tasks for the day, such as scoring that day's Ladies Tournament, presenting prizes during lunch, and other duties. Her note also said that his dog, Kenzie, had taken his golf clubs to Terry's car and she was shopping somewhere. Later in the day he invited me to a 'voluntary mandatory rematch' and announced that I would be giving him more strokes.

— Laird Small, Professional Golf Instructor

THE FORTY THIEVES

Edgar played with a group of guys called 'The 40 Thieves.' They'd play in groups of eights and 10s, played well and really fast, and bet on everything possible. It was amazing how quickly they'd finish 18 and how much money went around, but nobody got fleeced. When Quail opened, Ed treated them to round after round because I think he made more on the bets than he would have on their green fees.

— Dan Tibbitts

Just like the Monterey Peninsula and golf, Arnold Palmer and the U.S. Open naturally go together. And here he is, the all-time great, getting in a few practice swings on the tee behind the Carmel Valley Golf and Country Club Tuesday morning. Palmer, who always stays at Quail Lodge when he's here for the Crosby, has lots of company in the Valley this time. Bob Charles, John Miller, George Archer, Don Klenk, Bob Zender, Rob Cerrudo, Doug Sanders and David Graham are also headquartered at Quail Lodge, taking advantage of a helicopter provided by the CVG&CC to whirl over to Pebble Beach without getting caught in any Carmel Hill traffic. (June 15, 1972. Photo by Jerry Lebeck.)

THE OLD MAN IN A CAST

I recall following my dad during a state amateur tournament in Pebble Beach. He had broken his left foot and was hobbling around on a cast using a golf club for a cane. He looked like he could barely make it to the tee box. His opponent was a young golfer about 30 standing 6'4" high and weighing about 240. The kid looks at his buddies and smiles as he steps up and drives a long ball in the center of the fairway. My dad says matter-of-factly, 'Nice drive. Well done. I hope I can do as well.' Then he lays down the golf club cane and smacks one that flies 10 yards past the guy's ball. By the time the round was over, the kid just collapsed, disintegrated.

— John Haber Splittorf

MOMENTS

THE POACHER WHO KNEW THE BOSS

When golfing with the boss, nobody every got in the way. One day we caught up with a single, who never had status on a golf course, and we didn't recognize him so we asked if he was poaching. He replied nonchalantly, 'No, I'm playing and I'm a friend of Ed Haber's,' Well, Edgar was standing right there and burst out laughing. As we drove off Edgar said, 'Well, thank you, but I don't think we've met; have a nice game.'

— Ralph Drumheller

SNEAKING A ROUND

Mr. Haber had a floor-to-ceiling window leading out to a narrow walkway near the stairs. Sometimes I'd see him sneaking out through the window with a golf club in his hand. Nobody knew where he was and Nancy wouldn't tell, but there he'd be, on the range hitting balls. For him everything seemed to be centered around playing golf.

— Mike Ochs

SAD BUT HAPPY

The scariest experience I had with Edgar was when I applied for the head professional job at Spyglass. At the time his mindset was if you weren't 100% involved with Quail, you should be looking for a job elsewhere and your resignation pay check was at the end of the day, not two weeks hence. The job at Spyglass was big, a national job. I hemmed and hawed about talking to Edgar about it and, to my great relief. Somehow he had heard about it and siad, 'Go ahead, you should do that,' so I went to the first interview, then a second and finally the third when they offered me the job. When I told Edgar it was one of the hardest things I'd ever done, he said he was sad but happy for me. Relieved, I was able to leave without the regret of his displeasure.

— Laird Small

7 SKINS, 7 GUYS, NO FRIENDS

I joined in 1979 and didn't have a lot of time to play golf, and my high school golf game was long ago. But Edgar asked me to play with a small group that had evolved after the notorious Friday Bandits. On the first tee, he was a master negotiator; so good, some say, that he had the round won before hitting his first drive. I was but a rank amateur in every way, and had to work hard to negotiate for as many strokes as I could get.

Seven guys were playing in the group and seven skins had accrued by the time we reached the 3-par 17th hole. I was playing with an unflattering 18 handicap — a stroke a hole — including the par threes, which isn't very manly. Not much of a threat to anyone.

My drive spurted wildly into the right bunker. I slipped into the bunker and blasted a powerful shot that spurted the ball in a hail of sand onto the green where, somehow, it slithered slowly into the cup for a birdie that, after deducting my stroke, was scored as an ace on the card.

I was bursting with the excitement after holing a sandy-birdie and expected enthusiastic congratulations, but there was dead silence as the others trudged to the 18th tee box. It wasn't until a festive 19th hole with lots of drinks that I was presented with the bar bill. I learned I'd earned 49 bucks on the shot only to lose it all on some other kinds of shots. I learned that glory on the golf course was relative: forever memorable but short lived.

— Gary Koeppel

GOLF: THE GREATEST GIFT

As I age I appreciate more just how golf can extend a lifestyle with a quality of life otherwise unknown or unequaled; to have fellowship by golfing with friends, which may be the greatest gift of all. Quail is Edgar's gift to generations to come and enjoy one of the greatest games ever invented. It's only a game, a silly game of trying to knock a tiny ball into a wee hole with a stick. It's not a game of life or death, it's far more important because it reveals exactly who you are. That's also why it's such a great game for business because it gives you the opportunity to see someone's qualities outside of business. We are the beneficiaries of Edgar's vision, energy and generosity, which secure his place in our hearts as a most incredible man.

— Ducky O'Toole

SWEET SHOTS

THE PERFECT SWING

I'm not a golfer but our pro at the time, Laird Small, told me once if I wanted to see a perfect golf swing, look at Ed Haber's, because it was the same every time, regardless of how far out he was or what club he used, it was just the same swing every single time. So I asked Mr. Haber how he got such a consistent golf swing and he said, 'Well, when I started to play golf, I didn't have any money so I had to hit into a canvas bag in the back of a golf shop for a year and a half before I went out and played the San Francisco Open. If I hasn't perfected it, I would still be there.

— Steve Gould

MAY I TRY YOUR DRIVER?

I tried to learn golf with a seven, wedge and putter, then finally bought a set that had some woods that were metal, not wood, and I couldn't hit a thing with them. We were at the 14th tee box where I had whiffed the ball two times when Edgar drove up and got out of his car, still limping from his hip surgery. 'Mind if I try that new club,' he asked? His drive cleared the last sand trap on the right and went clear into the executive villa, which astonished me because, with a recovering hip, he had outdriven Greg Norman, who I'd watched the week before during the Spaulding Tournament.

— Steve Gould

THREE IN THE CRAPPER

At one time or another, my Mariachi band has played for everybody everywhere around here from Bing's Clambake to Edgar's classy shindigs. One afternoon at Quail during the Doris Day animal benefit, to raise some money for animals, I think it was Clint who egged Ed on to chip some golf balls at a small, one-hole portable outhouse about a hundred yards away. Ed Haber wasn't a show off, but to be a sport he finally said okay, picked up a nine iron, dropped three balls on the ground and chipped all three right through the door and into crapper. Darnedest thing I ever saw. The guys who bet against him wound up giving Doris about a grand for her animal charity deal.

— Mike Marotta

BY THE OLD OAK TREE

In about 1957 I was only six when my dad built a house on Mira Monte. He used to chip balls at a small hole in the base of an old oak tree about 125 feet from the back lawn of the house. He was a pretty good golfer and we kids would watch him and shag balls. We picked a lot of golf balls out of that two-foot hole. He seemed to hit them exactly where he wanted them to go.

— Warren Haber

BEN DOYLE

THE GOLFING MACHINE

Homer Kelley's famous 1969 yellow-covered book titled The Golfing Machine is indelibly linked to Quail Lodge because the club's long-time golf instructor, Ben Doyle, was the first professional to be given a copy of the book by Kelley and the first licensed instructor of the technique. Ben came to Quail in 1973 and brought much acclaim to the club by teaching the technique to Bobby Clampett and to golf instructors who traveled to Quail from all over the world.

— Ross Kroeker

FLAILING FOR LEVERAGE

Mr. Haber was a very good golfer. He hit the ball clean, anti-divot. He hit up on the ball instead of hitting down on the ball. He was a very good athlete and he learned to flail the ball to create leverage.

— Ben Doyle

GOLF ON THE BEACH

I was teaching at the Johnny Miller Golf Camp at Laguna Seca when I called Edgar about the opening for a golf pro. A young golfer named Holmes was also applying, but he didn't like kids, so Edgar suggested for him run the pro shop and for me to teach. When he said he doubted if I could make a living teaching. I told him I could make a living teaching golf on Carmel Beach. He agreed and offered $300, but after my first day he upped my pay to $400.

— Ben Doyle

HABER'S GOLF KIDS

Mr. Haber gave hundreds of kids the opportunity to learn how to play golf. He let all the local high school golf teams practice and play with free balls and range time. He provided the course for all of the school team championships.

— Ben Doyle

THE NOT-SO-MAGIC MARKER

Once Ben Doyle was giving golf instructions to a challenging lady student and, using one of his many unorthodox but effective methods, he wrote on her golf glove with a magic marker pen. Later the husband made a big stink because he had just bought his wife the glove. When Mr. Haber heard about it, he said 'Just send her another glove and he'll get over it.' He knew Ben was a great golf instructor and was as if he was saying, 'He can do what he's doing…just let him do his thing.'

— Jeanie Gould

THE DEVIL'S IN THE DIVOT

Golf instructor Ben Doyle was big on the 'impact zone,' that is, hitting down on the ball and then scooping a divot, a technique that drove Edgar nuts. The practice range was visible from the upstairs bar and dining room, and the divots would spoil the beautiful scene, a big part of what he and the guests enjoyed. When having lunch he'd often call down to the pro shop and ask for someone to replace the divots. He finally asked Ben to move to the far end of the range where the divots could not be seen as easily from upstairs.

— Laird Small

THE COCONUT LESSON

Mr. Haber encouraged Dwight Morrow, owner of the dairy farm on which the golf course was built, to learn how to play golf and he asked me to teach him. Mr. Morrow would say during a lesson, 'Ben, you got to get that into my coconut,' meaning his head, an expression that was picked up by many members in the club.

— Ben Doyle

DIVOTS AND ANTI-DIVOTS

Mr. Haber didn't like divots. He was anti-divot. And, of course, when I came along, I was pro divot. And so, after the days' lessons, my students and I had taken a lot of divots. Mr. Haber would come out in the evening and replace the divots. And I never did because I knew that's what I'd be doing all the time, replacing divots, so every day I had the grounds crew bring a cart of soil and cover up the divots.

— Ben Doyle

Golf Shots, Short

*A missed shot is not the
end of the world — unless
it's the last putt
on the 18th and you
lose the match.*

— Edgar Haber

Humor needs no explanation, so the following anecdotes stand on their own funny legs without introduction or comment.

IT TAKES TWO, YOU KNOW

One day by the lake on the 14th fairway I remarked on the beauty of the large grey heron that had just majestically landed. Then, on the lake on the 15th fairway, I saw another grey heron and said to Edgar, 'We just saw him on the 14th, could it be the same bird?' He looked at me with that deadpan expression and replied, 'Well, it takes two, you know.'

— Gary Koeppel

POOL PASS FOR PRETTY LADIES

Mr. Haber would often hand out pool passes to attractive women. When asked why he did that, he replied, 'It's just good for business because if there are nice looking women out there there's going to be some nice looking views,' then added, 'And I have a very good view of the pool from my office!'

— Jeanie Gould

NEGOTIATE FIRST, THEN PLAY

Edgar's golfing buddies suffered gallantly from his enduring and enviable skill — both as a golfer and as a masterful negotiator, angling for strokes and wagers on the first tee. Some even say he negotiated so well that he won the match before the first ball was even struck.

— Robert Sageman

THE QUAIL WEATHERMAN

I moved here as a sportscaster for CBS Television News. Every night during his forecast, the station's weatherman, Carl Bell, would announce the local temperatures in 'Seaside, Pacific Grove, Monterey, Carmel and Quail Lodge.' Carl told me one day while golfing at Quail, Mr. Haber told him, 'I watch you on TV but I don't want to give you all the credit for your weather report because you happen to live in heaven on earth here and the weather deserves at least half of the praise.'

— Hunter Finnell

PLEASE TURN OFF THE FROG TAPE

When my husband was the assistant general manager of the Lodge, a guest from New York, who booked her room for a week, called him at home about 2:00 in the morning saying she couldn't reach anyone at the front desk and asked, 'Will you puleeze turn off the damn frog tape?' Steve explained the sound came from real frogs and he couldn't turn them off, but Edgar heard about it and in the middle of the next night some staff were bagging and moving the frogs to a nearby pond until she left.

— Jeanie Gould

VAGUE MEMORIES OF NEVER WINNING

I enjoyed many rounds of golf with Edgar at Cypress and Quail, but I can't seem to recall ever winning a round or collecting a wager!

— Bob Sheppard

WHEN A BRIS IS NOT A BRIE

Ed told me his parents were Jewish but he was raised as a Christian, so when his Jewish daughter-in-law gave birth to a son and invited him to the Bris ceremony, he didn't know what to do. He said, 'I'm going to attend, you know, one of those ceremonies, what do you call it, a Brie?' And I said, 'No! It's not Brie. Brie is a cheese, for God's sake. It's called a bris.' So he says, 'A bris. So, what do I do, I mean, what do I do?' I said, 'You want to be a hero?' He said, 'I always want to be a hero.' I said, 'Look, when the rabbi completes the circumcision, be the first one to stand up and say, Mazel tov!' He says, 'Molotov?' I said, 'No, no, I said mazel tov.' I said, 'say it again,' and he repeats it and asks, 'What does it mean?' I said, 'It means good luck!' So he says, 'Mazel tov, mazel tov.' So the next time we played golf on the following Friday he says, 'Sam, I can't thank you enough. As soon as it was done, I stood up and yelled Mazel tov and every looked at me and applauded!'

— Sam Trust

THE LOG FOUNTAIN

In 1964 when digging the foundations for the lodge, we uncovered a large redwood burl. The Habers wanted to use part of it for a fountain in the entry to the new lodge. But when I hauled the log to an old sawmill in the village, the two brothers, who spoke with a thick German accent, began arguing about how best to cut the log to please Mr. Haber. I was standing beside a large spinning saw blade as the argument got hotter and I began imagining a fight with severed arms and legs flying all over the valley. Eventually, to my relief, they got tired of arguing and cut up the log the way Edgar wanted it and I left with all my limbs intact.

— Charles Haugh, Project Landscape Architect

THE TWINS

Edgar was always a gentlemen but he always had a sharp eye for attractive ladies. We couldn't afford the ticket price, but the Haber's invited us as guests to sit at his table for a New Year's Eve black tie ball. I bought a new dress — rather low-cut for a mom — and so we got all duded up. (By this time we had known and worked for the Habers for several years. He had even let me bring my baby to the office because we couldn't afford a sitter). As the Habers walked in Edgar looks down at me and says, 'Where have you been hiding them? You've never introduced me to the twins before.' When Terry said, 'Edgar, you're drooling,' he replied, 'Well she never dresses like that in the office!'

— Jeanie Gould

SOUR MASH AND WHIPPED CREAM

Every year Quail hosted many tournaments, one of which was rather memorable, though a bit risqué. There were bare-breasted Bacardi girls on each tee box pouring rum drinks and dispensing cans of whipped cream for, ahem, obvious uses — and in broad daylight! I asked my husband Steve, who was the assistant GM, if I could attend the annual banquet with him, to which he adamantly said no. I kept asking and he finally relented, but with the strong stipulation that I could not tell anyone I was married or was his wife because no spouses were allowed. So at the party I was introduced as, 'this is Jeanie from PR.' That was part of the deal, I had to lie in order to see what the party was all about, but when I found out, I got out of there very quickly. Oh, my.

— Jeanie Gould

THE FORTY THIEVES: AN INVESTMENT OPPORTUNITY

The Forty Thieves was the nickname given to a group of golfers whose games began in the 1960s at Pebble Beach and migrated to Quail as soon as it was open for play. They were men from all walks of life who had a penchant for business opportunities and who played golf in order to develop their business interests on the course. Yea, they'd meet around noon three times a week, have a bite of lunch then gather at the first tee. Each player would have the opportunity to invest a little or a lot, according to his financial position and appetite for risk. The entire mob of investors would divide and gather into groups of four, five and six, then strike out to make and break their investment fortunes, after which they would retire to the gentlemanly confines in the back of the clubhouse to continue investing in the opportunities available in the game of gin.

— Lawson Little

THE ABALONE PROPOSAL

I proposed to my wife at the elegant Covey Restaurant at Quail Lodge, its only culinary equal at the time was Club 19 at The Lodge at Pebble Beach. Ernie, the popular waiter who had been attending tables at The Covey from the day it opened, served the engagement ring on a velvet cushion in a silver domed platter. My newly betrothed was duly impressed and I was pleased about myself and how it all went. The following day I walked into Edgar's office and proudly announced that I had proposed to Emma last night at The Covey. Without batting an eye he looked up from his desk and asked, 'What did you have for dinner?' I was taken slightly aback but responded that we had splurged and indulged ourselves on champagne and abalone. 'Abalone?' he repeated, 'Well, you can get engaged anytime, but you can't eat abalone very often!'

— Gary Koeppel

CART DOG FOR A MATE

I wrote about Haber many times in my column in the <u>Chronicle</u>, but once on his birthday I wrote this to him: 'Over the years you've learned how to crash golf carts, respond to fires, import goats, avoid poison oak, be the unofficial Mayor of Carmel Valley, negotiate for free helicopters and, because humans refused to ride in your cart, when you play golf, only your dog agrees to be your cart mate.'

— Art Rosenbaum, feature writer, <u>SF Chronicle</u>

Puttering Around

The tree behind the 16th green overlooking the 17th hole is my favorite spot on the golf course.

— Edgar Haber

During the extensive interviews of more than 80 people who knew Edgar for this book, none were more delightful in their comments than the former pro golfer who ran the pro shop for the Habers from 1973-1984, all 11 years of which were during Ben Doyle's 40-year tenure as Quail's signature golf instructor.

In fact, Bob Holmes' comments about some of Edgar's lack of ability to relate to mechanical things were so funny and well narrated, they appear below in their original story-telling manner.

SOME REMARKABLE AND NOTEWORTHY EXPLOITS OF THE NOT-SO-MECHANICAL GOLFING GENIUS

A MAYNARD ON THE LOOSE

Here's another story about Edgar dealing with mechanical devices and his inability to figure them out.

Back in 1975 or so, a person came into the pro shop who invented, I think he invented this device, it was called the "Maynard" and it was a single-person golf caddy, an electric caddy that you could steer by remote control that Edgar thought was really neat.

So he said, "I want my clubs on that, I want to go try it." So we were out here in front of the pro shop at the time and he put his clubs in and he just got a new graphite-shafted Baffler club that someone gave him, which was a big deal in '74, a graphite shafted golf club…very expensive and it was a little bit oversized so it stuck out higher than his driver, jutting out about two inches higher.

So anyway, he gets the controls and starts the machine, he's diddling around with this thing, chasing anyone around the area like a kid, and this goes back to his inability to interface with electronics and his reputation as a mechanical klutz. And so he's making it go back and forth, then as he fumbles with the electronic control device, it careens and lurches right toward the pro shop, then

with a "bang" like a howitzer strike, the protruding object in the golf bag, the Baffler, smashes through the pro shop window, smashing it into pieces and breaking the club in two parts, but the Maynard had no intention of stopping, so several of us grabbed for the controls and calm was finally restored as Edgar sheepishly departed from the scene without so much as an editorial comment. We're still laughing about that one.

CODE 3 ON A HARLEY

He had just gotten his red light and siren on his station wagon, the Quail Lodge station wagon. He tried real hard for that, politicked hard…finally got it which was near impossible for a lay person to have a red light and a siren and badge to go with it — which was his fireman's badge.

And, at any opportunity — there could have been an accident in Prunedale or further, it didn't matter — and he'd want to go over there and direct traffic and go with his red light and his siren. Apparently he wanted to be a fireman or a cop or something.

Anyway, he's playing out on the golf course and radios had just gone down. We used to have these fancy radios that would go around the property, Motorola radios, and somehow he had forgotten his, or it didn't work, or whatever else, and so somebody had called down from upstairs and said, "You've got to go get Mr. Haber, there's an accident on Carmel Valley Road." But, of course, they couldn't reach him so it was up to me.

The only way to go get him, because you can't drive a car out onto the golf course, is to drive this 3-wheel Harley scooter, a utility cart that we had. It had handlebars, it didn't have a steering wheel…had handlebars and it had a clutch and a gas pedal and it was old and it couldn't hold water or dirt or anything else; it would all spill out…it was a real rat trap.

It was an awful machine. So I get on there and I haul butt out to the golf course…I backtracked him and I finally find him on 18th tee. And I say, "Mr. Haber, we've got to go, there's an accident on Carmel Valley Road and you're needed there. So let's go." So he goes, "OK."

He looked in the bed of the Harley and decided that wasn't appropriate, so I said hop on next to me. So, he hops on the seat, and it was a seat for one because you couldn't ride in the back. If I went over a bump, I'm liable to send him 40 feet in the air; it was that crummy of a machine.

Well, this seat was barely big enough for me and I was getting a vague feeling of impending doom, but off we go. We were each half on this seat thing but we weren't going too fast because I had left it in second gear, mainly because I didn't know there was a third gear.

So we tool down the 18th fairway and we come up past the green on 18, and have to slow for the curve there going up the hill and we go across the bridge there. And he goes, "I'm not comfortable." And, I said, "Well, Edgar, we are both not comfortable. This is an emergency, so just do the best you can. Hang on."

As we near the hairpin turn from the cart path to the parking lot, Edgar re-positions himself so he could lean into the turn. In doing so, his left foot tromped on the gas pedal and we lurched ahead as fast as second gear would allow. Down the turn we go, the engine screaming like a P38 on a bomb run, me hollering to Edgar to get his foot off the gas, and that vague feeling of doom I had was replaced by sheer dread. The more I leaned into the turn to counter balance the three-wheeler, the harder Edgar pressed the gas.

And so we're going down there and I said, "Get your foot off there." He goes, "Where, what?" And he's on there and we're going around that corner. We make the first corner, right turn. And then we go…he got his foot off of it, then we go to the right to make a left turn and he squishes over and squishes me over and somehow his foot hits the gas pedal again and we're on two wheels now, heading straight for the pump, the big pump that waters the entire golf course, that big. And I'm going, "We're dead. We're going to die here. I'm screaming, he's screaming, the Harley's screaming, and we're going to die! We're absolutely going to die."

And, so, we're on two wheels and I'm turning this thing as hard as I could because centrifugal force is throwing us right into this pump, with its knobs and pokey things all over it, it's just an awesome looking hazard. Anyway, I say, "Edgar, get your foot off." So he finally gets his foot off, we slowed down and negotiated the hairpin turn on two wheels, but when the other wheel comes down, we are now airborne, about a foot off the seat, and so we get back on all three wheels.

We arrive in front of the clubhouse. We make it. The Harley stops. We're both shook up. We can hardly walk after that; our knees are shaking. And we both look at each other like we had just seen Jesus. Off he goes to the fire and off I go to the clubhouse to change my shorts.

JUST ONE BUTTON AND...BOINK!

Well, Edgar and mechanical things. We had made a great new purchase down in the pro shop and it was this expensive NCR cash register that had all the bells and whistles of the era; it had buttons everywhere, about 200 or so, very impressive. And, a man named Tony from Salinas Cash Register was trying to explain it to us.

And, he goes, "Here you do this, and then you go here. And this thing is absolutely foolproof. You cannot make a mistake on it. It's got redundancies and backups…it's a wonderful device. It's top of the hill and it will keep track of your inventory and automatically subtract and flag it when you need new items because inventory is low and it's just a wonderful thing."

And, so he says, "I want you all to try it now." So, we're all punching it and it works fine and everything. After about an hour of intensive, hands-on testing by the staff, it truly was fool proof. He asked and everyone tried everything they could think of to make the machine make a mistake but all efforts were unsuccessful.

As the salesman/president was about to leave, Edgar strolls in to see what all the excitement was about. We related what we had been through and he seemed impressed. He asked if he could try it and we all thought it was a good idea.

And he says to Mr. Haber, "Why don't you try it? Don't worry, he laughs, you can't mess it up."

And he says, "Well, I don't do well with things like this." And so he goes, "It's absolutely foolproof, Mr. Haber." So Edgar goes, "OK." And he pokes one button.

There must have been 200 buttons on this thing. He pushes one button at random, pushes it and the whole system shut down, just quit, flat out. One button! Out of so many buttons, you couldn't do that on purpose. And he touches one button. "How about this one?" Boink, and the machine just shut down. No bells went off, no message popped up. Nothing.

Tony tried for an hour to get the thing working again, then he just gave up and said, "Oh, I'm going to have to take this back and reprogram it." That was the last we saw of him.

Edgar absolutely had a way with mechanical things.

RIDING THE MOWER

This was when Kevin Neely was the superintendent and that day, while we were out playing golf, a new device was delivered for mowing the rough. It was kind of a flail mower only it wasn't. It was like a gigantic rotary mower, the flat kind, but it had three blades on it and it would just mow down the rough and Edgar thought, "Oh, I've got to try this."

And right away I go, "Well I better go with him because he's going to cut himself in half or something. It's not going to be good." So, he's out there and says, "Let's go try that." And I go, "Oh, OK." So, it was on the 10th hole that night, it was in the winter time, and that evening the temperature got down to about 28 or 29 degrees, dark as can be, but this thing had lights and so we figured we could do it.

He goes out and he's driving it up and down the hills and he's getting so he's almost perpendicular to the ground on that right-hand side of 10 where it goes up the hill and he's up like this but it had a little sissy wheel on the back so you don't flip over and he was back on that thing, "Isn't this great, isn't this fun?" I go, "Yea, Edgar, let's don't do that anymore." So he goes, "OK, just a few more." So we go down. Finally we go and park it.

Edgar Haber, Chief Quail aka The Eagle, on Quail cart #1.

The next morning the superintendent comes in and he is livid and we're going, "What happened? What's the matter?" And he goes, "Have you seen the 10th fairway?" And we go, "No." And he goes, "Somebody took a mower up there and broke…all the grass was frozen, there was ice on the grass, and tore up the whole fairway. It will take months before that grows back."

And so, we're kind of going…and he knew who did it but you can't yell at the boss. He could yell at me, but, like I didn't know much about it. He was like a little kid and he enjoyed fun things like that. "This will be fun. This will be a nice ride." No, Edgar, not a good idea.

THE NAKED INTERVIEW

In the old days, Edgar used to have confidants and one of them was Burt Nishimora and Burt was the father of one of my best friends, Alan Nishimora, we went to high school together. And Burt was in the 442nd Infantry, the "Go for Broke" group and so Edgar would ask his counsel every once in a while.

Well, I heard through the grapevine that the current head pro, Lee Martin, was going to leave Quail so they were going to need somebody else. At that time I was working up at a public fee course in Santa Clara and so I hotfooted it down to Quail Lodge in hopes that I would run into Mr. Haber and say I'd like to apply for the job.

Somebody said he was down in the locker room, so I go down in the locker room and there's a naked guy standing there, kind of slim, holding his swimming trunks and I recognize him. And, I says, "Gee, Mr. Haber, I'm sorry I caught you with your pants down, but I hear there's a job opening and I'd like to apply for it."

He loved a good sense of humor and he thought that was funny and so we set up a date when he would have some clothes on for me to talk to him about the job coming up. And, I was still working up in Santa Clara and he and Terry came up to look over the operation because one of the primary concerns of his was the cleanliness of the operation. He was a stickler for things looking first-class, right?

And it just so happened that the week before we had re-done the pro shop and it was sparkling clean. It was absolutely wonderful. And, he says, "Does your responsibility continue outside the pro shop or inside?" And outside there were papers around and cigarette butts and everything else and I said, "Oh, no, uh, uh." Which wasn't true but I knew what he was getting at. And, from then on, in case there was a surprise visit, everything was cleaned up. So that was the beginning of my search to get this job down here, which I ultimately landed six months later in 1973."

THAT SILLY-LOOKING GRIN

One of the fun things…I can see this grin on his face today. When he'd hit a shot exactly like he wanted to he'd turn and look at you like, "That was it, I got it, and I hit that one perfectly." And, he would never say I hit it perfectly, he would just give you that silly-looking grin that, "Man, I got that one."

I don't know how many times I've seen that grin and I just always thought it was hilarious. He could make me smile just by giving me that funny grin. And, he was a wonderful guy to play with because he was absolutely first-class all the way. No throwing clubs. I never saw him bang the ground in anger. I heard him say only a few cuss words, but he understood the game. He understood that it was pretty much out of his control…he had great control over the golf ball, but there was a lot of it out of his control. And that was difficult for him, but one of the challenges he faced as a young man when he won the San Francisco City on through when he played in the British Amateur, his golf swing never changed.

When he got older, he got hurt. He had to make a few small changes in his swing. He tore his rotator cuff, his right one I'm pretty sure, so he would have to let loose of the club down at the bottom of the swing with his right shoulder and he was back quickly after that operation. And his swing never changed from then on.

FIRST, YOU NEGOTIATE

And a competitor: he…in all these years of knowing him…he never got the worst end of a deal, ever. And that includes the first tee. He had it won before he put the tee in the ground. Because he knew what his capabilities were. Occasionally he'd take partners and he knew whether they were playing well at that time or not playing well and if they weren't playing well, he would negotiate for extra strokes. The best negotiator ever. He was just wonderful. If you were his partner, you were going to win.

THE FORTY THIEVES

And before I came, he used to have a group called "the bandits" and they would play Mondays, Wednesdays and Fridays. When Quail became a reality they played out here quite often, but they used to play other places and one of the people in the thieves, the bandits was Ray Parga who was the caddy master at Pebble Beach and his assistant, Roy, who was also working in the pro shop, and they were part of the 40 thieves. It was quite an eclectic group.

There was a plumber, a restaurant owner, a roofer, two guys who worked in the pro shop, just run-of-the-mill guys. As happens in golf, you're all the same when you're on the golf course and Edgar, that's the way he felt about it, too. Everybody's the same. I'm no better than you, you're no better than I am…we're golfers. And, in the old days, before Edgar had a lot of money, they used to tee off on the third hole at Pebble Beach because they didn't pay the green fees… ever. They would poach the golf course.

One of the many things I learned from Mr. Haber is that
once you step on the first tee, everyone is equal and
golf is bigger than any of us.
— Robert Holmes, Quail Golf Pro, Ret.

A POACHER'S POACHER

One day they were out playing, Edgar says he had a client, I think it was one of his insurance clients, he was in the insurance business, and he said, "Well, let's go over and play Pebble Beach." And the guy says, "Oh, you can get us on Pebble?" "Sure, yea. We'll go over here and hit a few balls first." And at that time, where the racket club is, tennis courts now, there was a little practice area over there in between the second tee and the third fairway.

And so they'd hit a few balls over there and Edgar would look and say, "Why don't we just drop a ball down here on the third fairway, we can just play from here so we don't have to walk way back there." Well, he kind of had a deal worked out with Ray Parga, Pebble's caddy master, however that day, Parga must have gotten up on wrong side of the bed or something and he goes out on about the fifth hole and he points to the three other people in the foursome and he says, "You didn't pay, you didn't pay, and you didn't pay." And he looks at Edgar and goes, "But you're OK. You're fine. You paid."

So he brings his guests out there and they get caught poaching the golf course. Here's the future head of Quail Lodge and the scion of Carmel Valley.

BUTTS AND BUNKERS

What a great guy he was and he administered by example. When he was out on the golf course, he would pick cigarettes butts up off the ground, rake every bunker that wasn't raked, and repair all divots. And he didn't have to do that, he could have hired somebody to follow him around to do that, but he did it. And, of course, watching him do that, you did it as well. And that's how he did it. Never told me to do it. But he would absolutely tidy up and liked his environment clean and pristine.

Late afternoon view from Edgar's favorite spot above the 16th green.

NO PLACE TO HIDE

Edgar firmly believe that there was no place to hide on a golf course. He says, "I never made any better arrangements or deals than I have on a golf course. There's no hiding out there. There's no subterfuge. And he told me when we first started playing together, which was a caveat for me, he said, "I can learn more about a man in nine holes of golf than years in a board room." And that is true. There's just no hiding out there. It's how you handle adversity; it's how you're a problem solver. It brings out the best in people and the worst in people. And so he would judge people and he would take all employees that were in a management position out to play golf if they were golfers. And he would do his assessment primarily by that.

BALLS IN THE BUSHES

We used to have the high school kids here but in order for them to play here and practice, they had to do some work. He was a real proponent of earning your keep. And, so the kids, in the afternoons would be responsible for going along the periphery of the driving range and dig out range balls that were in people's hedges or in the trees or buried…got plugged in the golf course…he would be adamant about they need to go out there and do this. And I would organize them, I'd say, "OK, you guys got to do this, got to do that." So they would do it.

And one time there were a couple of kids and they were picking the right side of the range, over where the houses began and one of the homeowners, who was new at the time, came out and raised holy hell that these kids were in his bushes. And they tried to explain to him and I tried to explain to him, "We're just trying to get the range balls out of there," but the man insisted, "This is my property and you can't be here!"

So Mr. Haber calls him up on the phone and the fellow says, "I don't care who you are this is my property and you can't do that." So Edgar instructed the superintendent, at the time it as Kevin Neely, to make plans for putting a 12-foot high fence up so the balls wouldn't go into his hedge. And this was to be a solid fence. And, he dug the postholes and put the 14-foot tall four-by-fours in, down two feet so it was a 12-foot high fence that would absolutely eliminate this man's view. He wouldn't be able to see out his back door where he used to see the hills and San Carlos Ranch and it was a gorgeous view in the afternoon with the sun setting…well, he wouldn't be able to see that any more with this fence going to go up. All he needed to see was the posts going up and that's all it took. He called up and said, "Gee, Mr. Haber, these guys are welcome any time over here and I'll even help them get the range balls out of my bushes."

IT'S OKAY TO FLEECE

Edgar was fastidious with his dress, his car, his home, and especially his decorum on the golf course. He grew up when gentlemen played the game and comported themselves as such. No needling or gamesmanship was allowed. If you showed someone up on the course by beating him, you needed to be gracious in your victory.

And a gentleman on the golf course, absolutely a gentleman…no swearing, no throwing clubs and no gamesmanship that wasn't subtle. He enjoyed subtle gamesmanship but anything overt like, "miss it" or "hope you shank it" or something like that, it was absolutely verboten.

One day a lawyer and good friend I have played with for 20 years joined Edgar and me for an afternoon round of golf. Things went swimmingly for 13 holes. The 14th at Quail is a dogleg left par five with fairway bunkers guarding the left hand side. Edgar teed off followed by my friend and then it was my turn. I pulled my drive a little and it looked as if it would make the bunker. My lawyer friend yelled, "Get in the bunker." I have heard that kind of talk before and it doesn't bother me, but Edgar gave me that look that said, "Did I hear what I think I heard?"

Nothing else was said until we paid our bar bill and Edgar asked me into his office. "Don't ever have that guy back here as your guest." Hmm. Now I'm in a quandary. It's Edgar's sandbox and he gets his way so what am I to do.

A year went by and I figured that was enough time, so I had the lawyer back and we were sitting in the bar when Edgar asked me to come to the office. Nothing ever good came from a visit to Edgar's office. Uh oh! I'm in for it now. What to do?

Thinking rapidly ahead, the only explanation I could think of was the simple truth, and would only be appreciated by someone who had a close relationship with a dollar. "I told you never to have that guy back." My reply was "Edgar, if I never had him back, it would cost me about 50 dollars in winnings each time."

He thought a second and said, "You're going to fleece him? OK, you're right. Bring him back anytime."

THE CULTIVATED GROUND RULE

And one time, we're playing the 7th hole and he had pulled his tee shot over into some, apparently there were some flowers or something fairly close to the golf course. I'm not sure if they were on the golf course, but they weren't out of bounds.

Anyway, his ball was in here, in those plants, and I said, "Oh, gee, that's a shame, Mr. Haber." We were opponents at that time. And he goes, "Well, I'm calling this is cultivated ground and I get a drop." And I said, "What?!" And he goes, "Yea, cultivated ground, it's in the rule book somewhere. Cultivated ground and I get a drop." And I said, "Well, I don't think so." And so he goes, "Alright, I'll play it." And he knew better. He wasn't trying to cheat; he was just trying to see if I knew the rule.

And, forever on after that whenever we'd get a bad lie he'd say, "Well that's cultivated ground." And that was the first time I'd heard it and the first time I think he'd said it and it carried on for the rest of his life. "That's cultivated ground!"

A COCKTAIL BEFORE NINE

We used to play the front side generally when we'd go in the afternoons and we'd play three, four times a week, nine holes in the afternoon and we'd get to the ninth tee and there was a gentleman who was friends with Edgar and friends with most of us and he had a condo there, so we'd let him know we were coming by and he'd have hors d'oeuvres and drinks and we'd stop there for 20 minutes and have a drink and salmon pâté and it was just really a nice set up.

Well, Edgar wasn't much of a drinker and, actually, he couldn't drink very much at all because it affected him differently. Anyway, if he was winning, we would all encourage him and we'd pour him a cocktail and I'd say, "Well you don't want to embarrass him and not drink it." "No, no, I should have this." So he'd do it.

I don't think he ever parred the ninth hole after that. And he knew what was going on, but he didn't care about the money.

MOVERS AND SHAKERS

And, as far as golf and meeting people, through him I met captains of industry, would take your phone call in the middle of a board meeting if you wanted to talk golf and he always felt the same way.

He got to know people, very large people in their respective businesses because he was a good golfer. And he said that is the most wonderful thing, getting back to what golf can do for you, and how you should respect the game. We had the presidents of Titleist, Amana Refrigeration, NBC, Dow Industries in Argentina — to name just a few — an enormous group of movers and shakers who would come here and play golf with Edgar because they knew he was a good golfer.

THE GOTCHA SCRAMBLE

I knew how to get his goat. And, he would appreciate a good "gotcha." Every Fourth of July, we'd put together a members' scramble. Edgar would occasionally play in some of those things and I encouraged him to get out there because, you know, he was a good guy as well as a tough negotiator and a pure businessman.

And, people need to see that part of him. And a good golfer and they would appreciate playing with him so I talked him into playing in this members' scramble where there's arbitrary foursomes made and mixed foursomes, men and women, and they would go out and have a common goal to play this scramble game which was real popular back in the '70s.

Well, there were three people who were members of this club who made 97% of the noise, complaints, gripes, bitches and headaches for Edgar. And they were all golfers. And so I go, "This would be hilarious."

And so, I typed up two pairing sheets; one with the correct sheet, who was playing with whom, and I had to take personalities into account that certain people wouldn't play with other people, so I jockeyed that around and I had a real nice looking pairing.

And then I made up one where he was with these three troublemakers. And, he called me from upstairs, and says, "Are the pairings made? Who'd you give me?" I said, "Well, they're made, yea, you want to come down and look at them?" He goes, "OK, I'll come right down."

So I went and pulled the correct starting sheet and put up this dummy one on the board that I had made where he's playing with all these people and he goes down there and he finally finds his name and he looks at it and his face starts getting red, because he was fair complected. I mean, his face got red and his ears got red and his eyes starting bugging out and he is upset.

"NO," he says, "you can't do that to me." And I say, "Why? What's wrong?" And he says, "You put me with those people." And I said, "Well, yea, it's good to get out and play with new people because I don't think you've ever played with them before and, you know, get to know the people." "How could you do that? Has anybody seen this?" I said, "Yea, it's been up for a couple of hours." And

then he's apocalyptic, he's just nuts and so I say, "Edgar, Edgar, here's the real one." And I set it up there. And he goes, "You…that was a good one, Bob."

4,500 FREE ROUNDS AND COUNTING

I was a sports writer for the *Carmel Valley Outlook,* and, of course, I'm always looking for a free golf round, so I called Mr. Haber up and I said, "Mr. Haber, I'm Bob Holmes…" "Oh I know you, you know, my kids…" "Yea, I know, I'd like to write a story about the golf club at Quail Lodge."

It was Carmel Valley Golf and Country Club at that time. Just getting started. And he said, "Well, sure, you going to write it up?" I said, "Sure, I'll write it up." So he says, "Come on out here and bring somebody if you want to and you can play."

So right away I just start teeing off on the first tee, there was not a clubhouse where we're sitting now. It was up in the yellow house where the condominiums are now between the 4th and 5th holes. And so I got to play a round there and he still has that article in his history of Quail Lodge that I wrote, it was quite a good article. But, I got a free round of golf out of it and that was the beginning of my 4,500 free rounds of golf I've played at Quail Lodge. Yea, this is a pretty good deal. What else can I do for you?

JUST PUTTING AROUND

He was the consummate golfer. He loved golf. We would go out…because the pro shop was down here…and spend a lot of time on the putting green, which I did, even though I was working. And Edgar would come down and if there was no game in the afternoon he and I would chip and putt and tell stories and yak it up and we'd do that for hours on end and it was fun and he'd go, "You know, this is the best practice in the world. Thanks for doing this." And I'd go, "I'm out of the shop, Edgar, I'm happy." And we'd play for quarters or 50 cents or whatever and we would work our way around. We did that for hours. I imagine there's a few thousand hours he and I were just putting and chipping on the practice green.

Edgar Haber with Dr. Paul Tocchet and Bob Holmes, part of Edgar's famous Friday group.

The Gift Of Giving

*On the 17th tee
I always tip my hat in
thanks for everything golf
has given me.*

— Edgar Haber

Of all Ed and Terry Haber's contributions to human kind, the greatest but the least known are their many philanthropic gifts to charitable organizations of every kind. Their donations were not in any way self-serving because they were all strictly anonymous. Only the recipients knew what and when they gave because the Habers never used their philanthropy for self-promotion. They insisted on anonymity and refused to have their gifts made public or their names used in advertisements or brochures. They shunned having their names appear as donors of a hospital wing or other recognition.

For them, giving was, simply, giving. Nothing more, nothing less. Albeit an act of kindness, it was first and foremost a gift for which they neither sought nor received any thanks, recognition or appreciation from others. Giving was their personal way of sharing the efforts of the financial successes of their labors of love.

A partial list of the charities to which they contributed is in the addendum.

GENEROSITY

During life one may meet a few folks who do more for you than you can ever do for them. Ed Haber's generosity to law enforcement has been without equal.
— John N. Anton, Superior Court Judge, Ret.

MILLIONS TO CHARITY

Ed and Terry sold Quail for a good price and made a lot of money, but not too many people know that, in fact, a very large portion of the sale proceeds they received went right into charity, millions of dollars, to be exact.
— Anthony Lombardo, Esq.

EDGAR'S SHORTCOMING

Ed Haber is a gracious man but has one real shortcoming. He politely chooses never to accept the credit he so richly deserves for all of his many contributions. The Valley and Peninsula communities will never know what deeds he has done and sacrifices made for them. But if you have to have a flaw, I guess that is probably the best one to have.
— James J. Hill, III

SHARING THE GIVING

You know, he imbued everyone with the feeling of being part of something marvelous and magical and beautiful. Okay, and something decent and good and superior, all right? Not just him but everybody who worked for us. And he tried to let people know what he felt. And he tried to let them know he knew when they were trying to help, too. He showed them by giving. Like when we shared our condo in Hawaii as an award for employees or when we had our Five-Star Award employee dinners when the executive staff did all the serving. Their heart was in it and he was willing to share his heart and his world with everyone around him, especially the employees. Unfortunately, he didn't share as much with his family, but he certainly did share with them everything that had to do with here. His kids will tell you that. I'll tell you that. But what was created here was beyond the physical structure; it was the feeling the employees had and shared with the guests who came here. They felt that genuine sense of friendliness.
— Terry Haber

Doris Day

Loni Anderson

Vicki Lawrence

ELEGANCE DAY WITH DORIS

In 1993 Edgar hosted and sponsored a benefit for Doris Day's Pet Foundation. In addition to the 650 attendees, some of the celebrated guests joining Doris Day were Clint Eastwood, Vicki Lawrence, Loni Anderson, Suzanne Sommers, Desi Arnaz Jr., Dean Stockwell, and the Beach Boys' Mike Love, Al Jardin and Bruce Johnson. The evening was capped of with a dinner-dance in an enormous tent hosting 950 people with the music provided by the world-famous Les Brown's Band of Renown. An enormous sum was raised for Doris Day's charity.

— Quail Trails, Winter, 1993

OPERATION CHRISTMAS CHEER 1

Operation Christmas Cheer was a charity program sponsored by the Salvation Army, First National Bank and the <u>Monterey Herald</u>. Near the end of his life Edgar Haber finally allowed the program to publish his name in hopes that it would encourage his many friends in the Peninsula to give more.

— <u>Monterey Herald</u>

OPERATION CHRISTMAS CHEER 2

My First National Bank and the <u>Monterey Herald</u> newspaper, in collaboration with the Salvation Army, began an annual charity program called Operation Christmas Cheer to provide money to buy underprivileged children toys and help their parents pay the rent or heating bill. So I approached Ed and Terry, who agreed to contribute generously on two conditions: that I get a matching grant and that the gift would remain totally anonymous. There are many generous charitable people on the Monterey Peninsula, but they usually wanted their name attached to something, but the Habers always stood out in my mind because they insisted never to have their name made public.

— Clayton Larson

OPERATION CHRISTMAS CHEER 3

Edgar and Terry gave away a lot of money to charities on the condition that the donations had to remain anonymous. He simply didn't want to take any credit for helping out. I remember after he passed, it was revealed that he was the anonymous donor for Operation Christmas Cheer. People were in shock that, you know… How much was it? They gave away almost $25 million over a period of time?

— Ducky O'Toole

EDGAR'S CHARITABLE CON

Ed phoned one day and asked me to go with him to the opening of a new animal shelter in Salinas. While driving back after touring the facility — and of course I should have known — he mused out loud, 'that was a wonderful place but they could use some dough, so I'm going to give them $5,000. Don't you think that's a great idea and wouldn't you be able to do the same?' Realizing I'd been conned but had little choice but to agree, I said, 'Sure, Edgar, I'll match it.'

— Anthony Lombardo, Esq.

Edgar and Terry Haber with Tony Bennett

HOW OTHER PEOPLE LIVE

The day before Thanksgiving, when Warren was six, Marilyn eight and I was 10, my father came home in mid-afternoon, which was unlike him, and said, 'I want you kids to see that not everybody lives the way we do.' He took us to a Safeway store and walked out with an overflowing cart of groceries. We delivered them to the janitor of the Equitable Building, his first project. I remember his wife and some little children with only one chair and a floor lamp in the living room. We unloaded the groceries and stayed awhile; they were overcome by the gesture. On the way home we realized how well we lived in our protected world in Carmel Valley — something I've never forgotten.

— Anne Haber

IT'S PERSONAL

Well, you know, Ed and Terry just felt that it was important to put together a Christmas party for the employees and to make sure that each gift was personal — and appropriate — for that particular person, including all of the children, whose gifts were sex and age specific. I think that was the difference. The Habers both had a personal touch and a personal relationship with everything and everyone. And always on their terms — personal. And, whether you were a PGA professional, the president of the bank or you were one of his busboys or bartenders, it was a personal relationship.

— Ducky O'Toole

DOUBLE YOUR MONEY, DOUBLE YOUR FUN

The Haber Cup Tournaments were a fine affair. Not only were they very competitive and a lot of fun for everyone, they also raised an enormous amount of money for charity, which was the purpose and entire focus of the event. One year, from a simple golf tournament, we raised $14,000, especially in no small part because at the end of it all Edgar always pledged to double the donations.

— Bob Evans

RANCHO CIELO

I was a sitting Superior Court Judge for many years and sentenced way too many delinquent kids who came from bad backgrounds and never had a chance. I wanted to create an effective alternative that would keep first offender youths from becoming repeat offenders. So I came up with a better idea, Rancho Cielo. Edgar was one of the first people to visit the 100-acres owned by the county that would make a great facility to give young men a chance. As a judge I knew nothing about business so I asked for Edgar's help because he and Terry had created a five-star resort out of a dairy farm in an anti-development community. He gave to us freely of his time and wrote us our first check — a big one.

— John Phillips, Superior Court Judge, Retired

TUITION

When I was 10 my divorced mother and I moved into one of the Quail condos and she asked if I still wanted to learn how to play golf, so she introduced me to Mr. Haber who let me practice and play in exchange for helping pick up balls. When I was 15, the word got around that my Mom couldn't afford to send me to Robert Luis Stevenson School and someone donated the tuition. That was Quail Lodge. That was Edgar.

— Bobby Clampett

Passing The Torch

When you spend most of your life building something that turned out well, and then it's time to pass the torch, it isn't the money you think about, it really comes down to the simple things like quality and trust.

— *Edgar Haber*

WHY WE SOLD TO THE PENINSULA HOTELS

"In the late '90s, when I was about 85, I was approached by numerous big hotel and resort chains and was actually hounded by some Japanese investors to buy Quail Lodge. I listened to all of them, but nothing felt right. After all, it took us 37 years to build and we didn't want to give it away to some stranger because Quail Lodge was our extended home and everybody who worked in our home was family. A family business with a family of employees, yes that too, but much more.

"Well, Terry and I finally decided to sell to The Peninsula Hotels because they are a first-class operation, world class, and quality. Their Beverly Hills hotel is a Mobil Five-Star, as we were for 20 years, so we knew they were solid, would run the place well and keep up the quality. Also, we had gotten to know Sir Michael and his lovely wife, Lady Betty, for about 20 years because he would always stay here during the Concours d'Elegance car shows at Pebble Beach. He's a serious car enthusiast, you know, with a collection that's out of this world.

"Anyway, I figured I could trust him to carry on what we had worked so hard to build out of that beautiful old dairy farm that my first partners helped me buy and then wanted to subdivide the place into 1,000 houses, a real shame, it would have really been very ugly, so I bought them out so we could keep the place beautiful. We planted over 150 acres of grasses, hundreds of trees and dug 10 lakes to make a golf course; we wanted to keep it nice, so we put the entire golf course into permanent easement so it could never be messed up, and the board chairman of The Peninsula Hotels knew that and felt the same way because he thinks long term, generations ahead.

"Well, that's kind of a long-winded answer, but in a word, it's because of who they are; there's nobody better in quality and service than The Peninsula Hotels. And that's why we sold to them."
— *Edgar Haber*

Edgar Haber on his favorite 17th tee.

THE SUCCESSOR

Sir Michael Kadoorie is a business executive and philanthropist who is chairman of The Peninsula Hotels and the China Light and Power Company. Most of their philanthropic activities are anonymous, but the Kadoorie Charitable Foundation, that offers greater opportunities to the disadvantaged, is one of the few that is publicized.

He is descended from Iraqi Jews originally from Baghdad whose family emigrated to Hong Kong and then Shanghai in 1880. He currently lives in Hong Kong with his wife, Lady Betty, and their three children, and they enjoy spending time in their Carmel Valley holiday home.

Michael, as he prefers to be called, has been awarded the French Legion of Honor, the British Knight Bachelor and Hong Kong's Gold Bauhinia Star, all of which are high degrees of merit granted by three governments for distinguished community service and philanthropic endeavors.

An eclectic individual, Michael collects rare antique vehicles, many of which he has restored. He is a frequent entrant of the prestigious Pebble Beach Concours d'Elegance classic car event and hosts The Quail: A Motorsports Gathering event in Carmel Valley. He is also a licensed helicopter pilot and founder of the leading providers of aviation services in Hong Kong, Heliservices and Metrojet.

Michael and his wife became frequent guests at Quail Lodge whenever they visited the area during the car events. They and the Habers became friends and had much in common: both Quail and The Peninsula Beverly Hills were recipients of the coveted Mobil Five-Star Award and both couples were major but anonymous philanthropists to numerous charities.

In 1978 Michael Kadoorie met Edgar Haber, quite by chance, and became close friends for the next 27 years. Michael is a charming, tongue-in-cheek storyteller who can spin a yarn-a-minute to fashion some hilarious tapestries, so in his own words are the following stories:

THE HELICOPTER HELLO

My first meeting with Edgar in 1978 was rather dramatic. I was in Los Angeles taking delivery of a new type of helicopter but it was very protracted because there were several new features needing installation by the same Hughes Helicopter engineers who had installed the ventilation system in Howard Hughes personal vehicle and had also worked on his Spruce Goose airplane.

So I was stuck there with my helicopter instructor and became impatient. I finally pried the bird out of them but didn't want to conduct the tests near the airport, so I rang Maggie Downer, my friend in Carmel, whose son had gone to school with me at the Institut Le Rosey in Switzerland, and said, 'Look, we've got an auxiliary fuel tank and Carmel is near the end of its range, so we want to come up and do the testing and a bit of training in your area.

The Founder and Successor in a 1912 Rolls-Royce Silver Ghost

Maggie called a friend who knew the owner of Quail Lodge and, in a short space of time, the president, Edgar Haber, immediately granted his approval to land on his property there because he was honorary sheriff, honorary fire chief, honorary this and honorary that. He was the first person to bring emergency medical helicopters into that area, so he had them flying in and landing all the time at Quail Lodge so a helicopter was nothing new for him.

In those days there was no GPS, so my instructor, Mike Smith, logged in the rough coordinates and we headed north. It was getting dark as we approached Carmel Valley and I had been told that Quail was on a golf course, so as it was getting dark, we eventually found and landed on a golf course; I could see a light waving with a hand coming toward us, so I got out of the helicopter and, to my surprise, fell headlong into a bunker up to my chest, which everyone later thought was very amusing, my being all of five foot two or so, and then I managed to climb out and walked toward this light, asking, 'Is this Quail Lodge?'

The man with the light said, 'No, it's three miles down the road that way,' he pointed. So we got back into the helicopter, which by that time it was pitch black, and flew west for a few minutes and landed here at Quail Lodge. Edgar was waiting with his automobile lights shining on the landing spot. Our helicopter happened to be in yellow and white, which were exactly the Quail colors at the time. Edgar was delighted. He drove us to the lodge in his car that was bristling with scanning radios that connected him with police, fire and everybody else who wished to talk, and Edgar seemed to be able to navigate and drive without the problems associated with trying to listen to three things at once.

That was my first meeting with Edgar and he could not have been more charming.

Sir Michael Kadoorie

COINCIDENCE IN CARMEL VALLEY

We took Edgar for a ride one day during our various tests and training flights and amazingly enough, on the third day a British person came walking over to our helicopter who happened to be a student of my helicopter professor, Mike Smith, a navy helicopter instructor, the instructor of Prince Charles. Can you imagine, connecting with an English helicopter pilot in Carmel Valley who was my instructor's student? It seemed like everybody I knew or wanted to know was somehow connected with this place, Quail Lodge.

FORMULA ONE AT QUAIL

Another remarkable coincidence happened at Quail Lodge. I am married to a Cuban and we have three children, so in thinking ahead about my kids growing up and speaking Spanish, I realized if there were ever a row between them, I wouldn't understand anything. So I planned a trip to Mexico for three weeks to learn Spanish. With only one week to go, my friend Chip Connor phoned and said I should come to Monterey where they had a racetrack and concourse event for automobiles. I told him I couldn't get away because my teacher was learning more English than I was learning Spanish, so right away he lured me here and again we stayed at Quail Lodge.

On visiting the track I met the Argentinean Juan Manuel Fangio, one of the greatest Formula One drivers in history. He didn't speak a word of English, so when we met I offered the few words of Spanish I'd learned and he was so pleased that he autographed something for me.

THE PINK TICKET STORY

Quail Lodge had become our place to stay when coming to the Monterey Peninsula. Many years later, while staying at Quail and attending the Laguna Seca and Concours d'Elegance car events, Chip Connor invited me to see Bob Lee's car collection in Sparks near Reno. He says to me, "We've been invited to see the cars and have dinner. I've a plane here and you're invited." So I said, "That's terrific, I'm delighted to come. Might there be room for Edgar, the proprietor of Quail Lodge? He's a man in his 80s and I think he'd love to come."

I called Edgar, who was still working at seven o'clock in the evening, and said, "you must ask your wife for a pink ticket for tomorrow night." He looked at me as though I was nuts until I explained, "In England, a pink ticket means you can go out for the night and as long as you're home in the morning, nobody asks any questions."

So he said to me, "Why would I be doing that?" And I replied, "Well, you've been included, Chip has a seat on the plane, and Bob Lee has an extraordinary collection of cars and there's dinner with it and we're going to leave at six and we'll be back here somewhere around midnight and we'll have had dinner with him and seen his wonderful collection."

And Edgar said to me, "You know, I can't go." "What do you mean you can't go, Edgar?" "Well, I can't go. There's $19.20 outstanding and we…" I said, "What do you mean, Edgar?" He said, "We close our books every night, there's $19.20…we don't know where that is and I can't close my books and I can't go."

I said, "Edgar, come, come." But no, he was adamant. Now, I was foolish at the time because I should have put a $20 bill in his hand, but I didn't think that quickly. So off we went without him. He sees me in the morning and he says, "Michael, I want to ask you something. How come you seem…you know, your family has interest in a number of things, you have a number of responsibilities, why is it you are able to, you know, go for the evening somewhere and here I am, stuck. I must be doing something not right for $19.20."

So I said, "Edgar, well, there's one thing and it's never too late to learn…it's called delegate. So may I suggest that you delegate and if you're lucky enough, you may get another invitation to go see Bob Lee's collection, but I can't promise you that, that's out of my hands but Chip will probably find a seat on the plane."

And I said, "More seriously, Edgar, we have a hotel in Los Angeles and if I can be of any help, we've got people coming through, accountants coming through, and maybe we can send you an accountant and he may be able to structure your books in some way where you're not going to have a headache and you may be able to come next time if you're fortunate to get another invitation."

So Edgar said, "Fine." And about two months later we did, we had people going up and down from Hong Kong so one of them came here. Well, then I didn't hear any more about the subject and that was the story of the Pink Ticket.

THE BEAUTY OF A HANDSHAKE

Like Edgar's experience in buying the property from the dairy farmer, who received a much higher offer after agreeing to accept Edgar's lower offer on a handshake, both myself and my father grew up on handshakes in a generation of gentlemanly people whose word was honorable and not something ever broken.

But things have changed with this generation because one deals with so many intermediaries before anything is settled in one form or another. I was fortunate to be brought up in that era but today that era is gone, which is sad.

We nearly lost the hotel company on a handshake. From one generation to another there was a handshake agreement with a partner who owned a considerable number of shares. Our handshake was that if they wished to sell their shares, they would come to us or if we wished to sell our shares we would give the other family the opportunity to buy them.

But the next generation came along, and even though we had the same handshake agreement, one day we leaned that the other person had sold their father's share, and worse, to some people who were green mailers, which as you know is a term cobbled from the words "greenback" and "blackmailers." That was an unusual but sad experience for our family. Fortunately, with Edgar and the dairy farmer, the handshake was between two gentlemen who honored their word.

PRIVILEGE BEGETS OBLIGATIONS

When negotiating with the green mailer to buy back his shares of our company, they were asking for a lot of money. I was quite a young man at the time, but I asked my dad, "What is the purpose of money if you are fortunate to have sufficient? You can only eat three meals a day. What you have to give is the opportunity for continued work with its obligations and to continue the family legacy." Our company had started in 1865 and we had been involved since 1920. It was a lesson about continuity, about what you have to pass to the next generation.

I enjoy what I do and although I am fortunate to have many privileges, with those privileges come the obligations. They say the first generation makes money, the second generation consolidates it and the third one loses it, so at age 70, I'm doing my best not to lose it."

Ducks in the Lake at the Lodge with the distant fountain.

MILKING THE STONE

Our company, which is public you know, has now owned Quail Lodge for the past 12 years and has invested heavily and lost heavily. I've battled with our board for the last six or seven years and have always been able to convince them that there is a future here, but we've had problems because of the economic downturn, some management issues and with the unions, but you can't milk a stone endlessly, so we'll see what happens, whether we can keep the property or have to let it go.

But, I'm quite certain that, however this pans out, and I don't know because I've steered clear of it for the time being, it will be for the best for Quail Lodge and if Quail Lodge is a success, as it must be, it should be a success for the entire community.

So our hope is to be able to continue Edgar's legacy, even though it cannot, or may not, be possible to do it directly through what Edgar handed over to the Hotel Company, it still must be done in the correct way and not the wrong way, and that's why it's taking so long to get it right.

It was not long after this interview that things at Quail Lodge changed dramatically. For 18 months the board of directors of The Peninsula Hotels circulated a request for proposal to find an appropriate new owner for the property. Several hotel entities inquired, two of which engaged in extensive due diligence and developed acquisition and renovation plans, but each were stymied by unsuccessful negotiations with the land lease owner who controlled the property on which two of the golf course holes were located.

Through a chance offer to introduce Sir Michael to the adjacent landowner and his subsequent purchase of the property, the land lease conundrum was finally resolved. Once again The Peninsula board was persuaded not only to retain the property but also to increase the capital investment by a reputed $26 million to be used for reopening the refurbished lodge and renovating the golf course.

A "photo op" shot from the 14th tee to the 18th green.

THE 2-HOUR SOLUTION FOR A 50-YEAR PROBLEM

In 2009 I interviewed Sir Michael Kadoorie for the purpose of writing this book. At the end of the interview, I told him I had heard he was considering selling Quail Lodge but the suitors had been discouraged by the owner of the land on which the 11th and 12th golf holes had been leased to Quail for the past 50 years; I had heard that the prospective buyers were having difficulty in negotiating a new lease. Quite coincidentally, I told him, a few months ago I had responded to a For Lease sign on the 39-acre property and had spoken with the owner, Mr. Russell Wolters, because I was considering starting a business on his 100% organic land called 'My Organic Garden,' which would rent old-fashioned 'victory lots' to individuals and restaurants for growing their own organic vegetables, but I had other priorities so I abandoned the plan. But I had met Mr. Russell and considered him to be a likeable and reasonable man, so I mentioned to Sir Michael that if ever he needed an introduction to solve the land lease deal, I would be happy to comply. Soon after the interview, Sir Michael phoned on a Friday afternoon and asked if I remembered my offer to introduce him to Mr. Wolters. Early the following morning I drove Russell to Sir Michael's home where, after two hours of amiable conversation in the Carriage House, an offer to purchase the land was made and accepted. The long-time, troublesome land lease issue had been put to rest for all time. It had taken Sir Michael two hours to solve the 50-year-old problem. As a result, The Hong Kong and Shanghai Hotels, Limited's Board decided to retain ownership of Quail Lodge and commit a substantial amount of new funds to renovate the lodge and golf course.

— Gary Koeppel

RESPECT FROM A STRANGER

I'm not sure I want this in the book, but it's a fact. When my father was negotiating for the sale of Quail Lodge to The Peninsula Hotels, I spoke with one of the people he was a friend with, Kadoorie, I think was his name. I said, 'You know, if my dad sells to you, he's going to need to be involved, somehow.' And he said, 'I understand, I truly do. My father is still involved in our business.' When Quail was sold, he kept his word and retained Edgar with a five-year contract and the title as the president of the company, despite no longer being the owner. When my father passed away, I wrote the Kadoorie fellow a letter and said how much I respected the fact he'd kept his word with me about my dad. I was surprised when I got a letter back, which I didn't expect, and thought that was pretty special for a person I didn't even know to have that kind of respect for my father.

— John Haber Splittorf

UNSUNG, UNKNOWN GENEROSITY OF SPIRIT

I held Edgar Haber in the highest esteem. He was a man who had made his own journey through life. He had reached the pinnacle — not only in terms of what he brought to the community with Quail Lodge, but in his own personal impact on the community at large in so many ways, many of them known and most of them unknown, especially for the generosity of his spirit. From a simple dairy farm he was able to envision, to conceive and build a really fabulous project; and I feel, in many ways, frustrated by not being able to fulfill my own hopes of continuing that legacy. He had a great personality and a remarkable way of bringing people together in the community. A man committed to the community, a man who could galvanize other people into action. I mean, he had a fire station built nearby that reduced the risk of fire for the entire community, he helped law enforcement that kept crime down and he helped so many people when rushing to their aid in that Mercedes of his with its flashing red lights. Indeed, he was a big picture person. He was a giver and it reflects. There wouldn't be a person in the community who would not have been touched by Edgar in some way. You could polarize his deeds around golf, but these things have nothing to do with golf; being a sheriff, a fire chief and all of that. This comes out of the deep good will of a person giving to the community he happens to live in. Betty and I are always amazed when we come here and see what Edgar and Terry created. We have a lot of respect for them and love f or the area. It's always a privilege to come here and enjoy the beauty. It is one of the most remarkable places on the planet and, thanks to the Habers, it is one of the best preserved and the most beautiful.

— Sir Michael Kadoorie

The Legacy

Upon Reflection

I began this book with the intent of memorializing Edgar Haber as the founder of everything that is Quail: a golf course, clubhouse, hotel and two subdivisions. But as my research evolved, I realized it was not Edgar alone, but also his partner and wife, Terry Haber, who together created all that is Quail Lodge; it wasn't the story of the man with the woman behind the man, but rather the man with the woman beside the man.

There are many people whose contributions are not included in this book because either I could not find them, they did not respond to inquiries or I did not know who or where they were. Undoubtedly, many who read this book will have their own anecdotes that, alas, are not included, stories that would have further enriched the portraits and added even more dimension to the Habers.

This book could not have been written without the anecdotes from those interviewed. Had their stories not have been included as direct quotes, readers would have assumed I invented the Habers as fictional characters and their accomplishments as imaginary achievements. But the contributors' stories are so convincing, as they say, that one simply could not have made them up.

I processed a few hundred anecdotes, memories and stories, but instead of assembling them on a flat surface as in a typical puzzle, I cobbled together the bits and pieces to shape three-dimensional portraits, more resembling sculptures than paintings.

It is gratifying to fulfill a promise made long ago to Edgar, Terry and myself. It is also satisfying to write a book about people who are so dimensional. But most of all, although the Habers have been personal friends for years, had I not written this book, I would never have been able to fully understand their many facets and successes as remarkable human beings.

Contributors

Ajan, Carmen
Ajan, Csaba
Anderson, William
Bayless, Mary
Beard, Henry
Blakeslee, Tim
Chapin, Don
Chapman, Bonnie
Chatterton, Roger
Christensen, Casey
Clampett, Bobby
Clampett, Mariana
Cook, David (Bud)

Day, Doris
Doyle, Ben
Drumheller, Ralph
DuVall, Pat
Eastwood, Clint
Etienne, Myron
Evans, Bob
Finnell, Hunter
Gould, Jeanie
Gould, Steve
Graves, Robert Muir
Graves, Victoria
Gray, Tom

Haber, Ann Isaacson
Haber, Candace
Haber, Edgar
Haber, John Splittor
Haber, Marilyn
Haber, Terry
Haber, Warren
Habermann, Norman
Hardesty, Clare
Haskell, Marty
Haugh, Charles
Heuerman, Jim
Hill, James J. III

Holmes, Bob
Holstrom, Brick
Kadoorie, Betty
Kadoorie, Michael
Kanalakis, Mike
Keene, Paul
Kerr, Denis
Koeppel, Gary
Kroeker, Ross
Langley, Jim
Larson, Clay
Little, Lawson
Lombardo, Tony

Marotta, Mike
Marquard, Skip
Nicklaus, Jack
O'Toole, Ducky
Ochs, Mike
Palmer, Arnold
Parsons, Nancy
Phillips, John
Quidleg, Rudy
Ragan, Art
Reade, Sydney
Reed, Ron
Rosenbaum, Art

Sageman, Bob
Salemah, Tony
Shephard, Bob
Silverman, Bob
Small, Laird
Smith, Gordon Paul
Talbott, Robert
Thigpen, Steve
Tibbets, Dan
Tocchet, Paul
Trust, Sam

Charities

Partial List

Alliance on Aging
Alzheimer's Association
American Red Cross
Boy Scouts of America
Boys and Girls' Club
Carmel Valley Youth Center
Carmel Valley Village Improvement
Community Foundation

Community Hospital Foundation
CHOMP
Family Services Agency
First Kid's Golf Program
First Tee
Food Bank
Gateway Center
Girl Scouts of Monterey Bay
Good Neighbor Emergency Relief Fund

Guide Dogs For The Blind
Hospice Foundation
Meals On Wheels
Monterey Bay Area Council
Monterey County Christmas Fund
Monterey Peninsula Corps
Natividad Medical Foundation
Operation Christmas Cheer
Planned Parenthood

Rancho Cielo
Red Cross
Salvation Army
Shelter Outreach Plus
SPCA
United Way
Violence Prevention Center
Women's Crisis Center
YWCA